**FELD MARSHAL SADDAM HUSSEIN
HERO OF NATIONAL LIBERATION**

IRAQ

A Tourist Guide

State Organization For Tourism
General Establishment For Travel
and Tourism Services

BAGHDAD — IRAQ • Telex — 2781 GETTS IK
Phone 7760026
P.O. Box 10028 KARRADH

1982

THE NATIONAL ANTHEM

In accordance with Decision № 851, dated 3—6—81, adopted by the Revolution Command Council, the initiatory music of the anthem entitled in Arabic Ardul-Furatain (Land of the Two Rivers), has become as of 17th July, 1981, the National Anthem of the Iraq Republic.

Music Note is Published herewith.

IRAQ'S NATIONAL FLAG

الجمهورية العراقية

EMBLEM OF THE REPUBLIC OF IRAQ

Summary

INTRODUCTION

Iraq, the Land of the Two Rivers, has a long history which gives witness to the greatness the country has known over the centuries in terms of human achievement.

Ever since man started to trade, Iraq has been a crossroad of caravans and commercial routes. Tourism has been a natural concomitant to such an activity, as an expression of man's wish to familiarize himself with the unknown and with the ways and manners of others.

Progressive, revolutionary and triumphant Iraq finds inspiration in its great history and the nation's magnificent heritage as it develops itself and builds up a better life for its people consonant with their yearnings and aspirations.

The Tourism Sector has been the object of distinct interest on the part of the Party's revolutionary leadership, which has ensured its successful growth by increasing touristic investments many times over what they were before the 17th—30th July 1968 Revolution.

Development in this respect was based right at the start on careful planning. The first step in this direction was a comprehensive survey of touristic potentials in Iraq, which led to the definition of the aims and means which made possible the drawing up of the 1975—85 Plan in two stages The Plan included the development of the present tourist facilities and establishments, and the improvement of their services for the benefit of national and foreign visitors alike. It also included the implementation of dozens of new projects, such as the construction of first-class and de luxe hotels in Baghdad and other towns in the country, and the creation of, for instance, the Habbaniya Tourist Village, one of the largest of its kind in the Middle East. The Autonomous Region in the north, so rich in natural beauty, received the intense attention of the State Organization for Tourism (S.O.F.T.) which has filled it with all the services and amenities that the visitor or tourist would expect to find for his comfort and delight.

The Tourist's Guide in your hands, dear reader, provides a true picture of some aspects of this country's great heritage and civilizations, its arts and sciences, its growth and progress, together with its tremendously varied landscape — from the palm groves of the central and southern plains to the snow-clad mountains of the north. We trust it will introduce you to the Iraq of yesterday's successive civilizations and the Iraq of today's progress and triumph.

The General Establishment of
Travel and Tourist Services,
Baghdad.

Iraq:
Geography
and
History

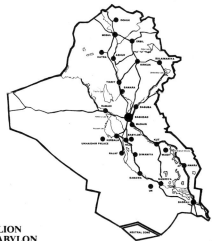

**THE LION
OF BABYLON**

GEOGRAPHY

Iraq, the cradle of civilization, is situated in the north-east of the great Arab homeland of which it is an important part. It lies to the north-east of the Arabian Peninsula, itself part of South-West Asia of which Iraq is an extension, because of their similar geophysical structures.

Iraq is in the southern part of the North Temperate Zone between latitudes 29.5—37.25 and longitudes 38.45—45.48.

It has an area of 438,446 square kilometres which includes the 18 governorates. In the central part, astride the Tigris, lies the great capital of Harun Al-Rashid, Baghdad.

Iraq is bounded on the North by Turkey, on the West by Syria and Jordan, on the South by Saudi Arabia, Kuwait and the Arab Gulf and on the East by Iran.

Because of its geographical position, it has been a bridge between three continents, Asia, Africa and Europe, and between the Indian Ocean and the Mediterranean. It is therefore, the shortest land route between Europe and South-East Asia.

The country can be divided roughly into three regions: the mountainous snow-clad north and north-east, about 20 per cent of the whole country, a central largely limestone plateau representing 59.5 per cent of the whole, and the southern flat lowland alluvial plain, with many lakes and marshes. Two great rivers, the Tigris and the Euphrates, traverse the country from north to south: their sources are in the far away uplands of Armenia and Anatolia, and they are fed by many tributaries, which makes Iraq notable for its rich water resources. The two rivers meet in the Shatt-Al-Arab, which runs through Basrah Governorate in the south to pour in the Arabian Gulf.

The Tigris is 1,718 kilometres long, of which 1,418 are in Iraq. The Euphrates is 2,300 kilometres long, of which 1,213 are in Iraq. The Shatt-Al-Arab, from the two rivers' confluence to the Arabian Gulf, is 110 kilometres long.

POPULATION

Iraq has a population of over 14 million, of which the majority are Arabs. There are several minorities which enjoy full national and cultural rights within the overall national framework of the Iraq Republic. Freedom to practise their religious rites is protected by law for all religious denominations, and their major feast days are official holidays for them.

The official language is Arabic, but there are also other officially recognized languages: Kurdish, Turkoman and Syriac. The foreign language most widely used is English.

HISTORICAL BACKGROUND

There are in the country about 10,000 archaeological sites in which lie hidden the remains of a long succession of civilizations that date as far back as the palaeolithic age, 100,000 years ago. The most recent are those that belong to the Islamic periods.

The cultural formation of the country was distinguished for its originality and continuity, which gave its civilizations a uniformity of its own. This partly explains why it was a focal point from which radiated sciences and arts that contributed to the progress of many parts of the world.

Iraq was one of the first regions in the world to create the bases of cultural and social stability. Eight-thousand years ago, in the neolithic age, villages were set up where man learnt farming, animal husbandry, housebuilding, weaving, pottery, and even the making of art objects by painting and sculpture. Jarmo, in Chamchamal in Ta'mim Governorate, is one of the earliest villages of man. In places such as Hassouna, Um Al Dabbaghiya, Matara and Tel Al Suwan, excellent finds have been unearthed which now grace museums at home and abroad. At Um Al Dabbaghiya, near Hatra, household paintings have been found that go back some 8,000 years. Tel al Suwan has given us a large number of superb small sculptures. It is interesting to note that Mesopotamian man, who lived in Shanidar Cave (near Arbil) nearly fifty thousand years ago, displayed a special sense of beauty: he strewed flowers on the graves of the dead — a thing never observed by archaelogists anywhere else in the world.

In the south, Al Ubeid civilization flourished almost six thousand years ago and spread out to the Arabian Peninsula and Iran. Half-way during the Age of Warka, 5,200 years ago, writing was invented in an iconographic form, which then developed into cuneiform. From 4800—4350 B.C. is the period known as the Dawn of Dynastics, which had three phases all distinguished for their remarkable artistry — evident in sculpture, seals, and the use of metals. The discoveries in the Royal Cemetery of Ur, in the south, give an idea of the high point of development the arts had reached in the 3rd millenium.

Later, under the Akkadians (2371—2143 B.C.), the country was united under a central authority which established the first empires in history. The Akkadians were the early Arab pioneers: their empire included Iran, Anatolia, and Syria.

For about a century after the Akkadians the country went through a recession caused by the invasion of a barbaric people across the north from Iran. Soon later, however, Sumerian princes emerged who resuscitated local culture, foremost among whom was Gudea, ruler of Lagash. From 2112 to 2004 B.C. the Third Ur Dynasty was established: its kings, especially the founder Urnammo and Shulgi, were noted for their love of art and literature. They left us their bronze figures which portrayed them carrying the earth-vessels they used in building — in expression of their participation with the people in construction.

The cultural chain continued The old Babylonian Age,

2004—1594 B.C., witnessed an activation of architecture, sculpture, seal carving, and especially literary arts and the sciences. In geometry and mathematics the Babylonians had formulated theories which were in much later times ascribed to Euclid and Pythagoras. They used 1st and 2nd degree algebraic formulae, and put the foundations of logarithms. Most distinguished, perhaps, were their humane laws — crystallized in the famous Code of Hammurabi (1792—1750 B.C.).

Assyrians, centred in the north, spoke the same language as the Akkadians and Babylonians and used the same cuneiform writing.

Historically, the Assyrians went mainly through three distinguished phases: the ancient (contemporary with the old Babylonian period), the medieval, and lastly the imperial phase, 910—612 B.C. They were remarkable for their love of building and their political organization: they founded the largest empires of their times and built great cities, such as Assur, Nineveh, Nimrud, Dur Sharrukin, whose remains are to be seen nowadays in museums throughout the world. The Assyrian imperial period was succeeded by the Neo-Babylonian age, 612—538 B.C., whose towering figure was the magnificent Nebuchadnezzar (604—562 B.C.). He was unique in his architectural and artistic achievements, together with his wise political administration and the skill and power with which he quelled all rebellious elements throughout his far-flung empire, which included Syria and Palestine.

Upon the fall of Babylon the country was dominated by foreigners: the Achaemenids, the Greeks (Seleucids) and others. They made use of the country's cultural heritage and expertise: Babylonians and Assyrians created many of the art works of Susa, Persipolis and Dazargaw. Their imprint was left on the sculpture and glazed bricks of those cities. The Greeks benefited from the Babylonian heritage of mathematics, astronomy, medicine, geometry and literature.

Two thousand years ago, or a little more, the Arabs made their architectural and artistic contributions in various places in the north, in Syria, in Jordan, in southern Anatolia. Their great buildings, statues and metallurgic works are still to be seen in part in Hatra, where they carved their names on their beautiful works. In Assur the Arabs, at the time of Hatra, built four great ewans, which still carry

15

the name of their Arab architect. Connected with the Hatra culture, before its demise in A.D. 241, was also the culture of Arab Hira, in central Iraq. Hira continued until the Arab Islamic conquest of Iraq in A.D. 632.

The advent of Islam caused a great revolution in many parts of the world. The people of Iraq, in cultural continuation, welcomed the new sublime message, and in embracing it they built a great civilization which, starting soon after the Prophet's Hijra, continued through the Umayyad Period, A.D. 660—750 and the Abbasid age, 750—1258.

Under Omar, the second Caliph after the Prophet, important cities were built, such as Kufa and Basrah. Under the Umayyads, Wasit was built as a link between these two cities, and under the Abbasid Caliph, Abu Jafar Al-Mansour, Baghdad was built in A.D. 762. Some sixty years later Samarra was built by Al-Mutasim in 836 to replace Baghdad as capital. In 892 the seat of the Caliphate went back to Baghdad, which remained the centre of government until its downfall on the hands of the Mongols led by Hulago in 1258.

The Abbasids' was a golden age: an age of wealth, learning and creativity, all patronized and encouraged by the caliphs themselves. Arab medicine, chemistry, geometry, mathematics, astronomy, poetry, all flourished — and were the greatest in the world.

Darkness fell upon the country after 1258 — Hulago, the grandson of Gengis Khan, left behind him a trail of horror and destruction. In the 16th century the Ottomans ruled Iraq — until 1917, when Iraq was placed under the British mandate. A form of political independence was at last obtained in 1932.

The people of Iraq have worked hard to rid themselves of the effect of centuries of stagnation. Their achievements have been truly spectacular.

**SPHINX FOUND AT FORT SHALMANSER, NIMRUD. 19 BY 15 CM
OVERALL**

2

Modern
Iraq

FORM OF GOVERNMENT

Iraq is a people's democratic republic. The Revolution Command Council, headed by the President of the Republic, is the supreme authority in the State. Resolutions are adopted by a two--third majority.

The Council of Ministers is made up of ministers heading the following ministries:

Defence, Foreign Affairs, Interior, Finance, Justice, Education, Labour and Social Affairs, Health, Culture and Information, Agriculture and Agrarian Reform, Housing and Developments, Planning, Trade, Industry and Minerals, Oil, Youth, Transport and Communications, Higher Education and Scientific Research, Religious Trusts (Awqaf) and Affairs, Irrigation, Local Rule.

INTERNAL POLICY

The Iraq Republic considers that the present stage is that of creating a national, democratic socialist system wherein government is the responsibility of a coalition front which includes all patriotic parties under the leadership of Arab Ba'th Socialist Party. The Progressive Patriotic Front was founded on 17th July, 1973.

Ministries and relevant establishments are responsible for the implementation of the resolutions adopted by the Revolution Command Council, which is the highest body in charge of legislation, guidance and supervision of actual execution undertaken by the executive authority, that is, the Council of Ministers.

Peoples's Councils, made up of the people's representatives, exercise their popular democratic function.

THE NATIONAL ASSEMBLY

The National Assembly, together with Revolution Command Council, participates in legislation. Its setting up has been an advanced step in the democratic building of the society structured by the 17th July Revolution: within the current phase it formulates the democratic practices of the masses alongside the other effective forms adopted by the Revolution. The National Assembly is based on certain principles, such as the absolute equality of all citizens, with the exception of those who take a hostile stand against the Revolution and revolutionary transformations, absolute equality of men and women, the rejection of formalistic practices of democracy, with emphasis on the serious content of democratic practices which express the principles of the Revolution and the seriousness of its method. In fact, the National Assembly embodies a pioneering experiment in the Arab revolutionary movement: it is an expression of the Arab nation's aspiration to build up its new life, guided by the principles of unity, freedom and socialism and those of the Arab Ba'th Socialist Party as well as the democratic revolutionary course adopted by the 17th — 30th July Revolution, in order to complete the setting up of democratic institutions and making them effective in the new society. In compliance with the political report of the Party's Eighth Regional Congress, the National Assembly is made up of at least 250 members freely and directly elected by secret ballot, so that it represents all the people of the Iraq Republic. The first elections were held throughout the country on Friday 20th June, 1980.

FOREIGN POLICY

In its foreign policy the Iraq Republic stresses abidance by the United Nations Charter, the promotion of good relations with its neighbours, its solidarity with the developing countries, and its support of the non-aligned group of nations. It maintains its help for progressive movements in the world, condemns racial discrimination, opposes old and new colonialism, confronts Zionism, and calls for the realization of peace and cooperation in the world.

Where the Arab nation is concerned the Party has been true to its national principles: the country's armed forces took an active part in the October 1973 War, Iraq used oil as a political weapon in the Arab nation's battle against its enemies, it gives unlimited support to the Palestinian Resistance and its struggle against capitulationary solutions and projects which aim at liquidating the Palestinian issue.

14TH JULY 1958 REVOLUTION

On the morning of 14th July 1958, the Iraqi army toppled the royal regime which had opened the door wide for monopolies to plunder the country's oil wealth under unjust concessions, tied Iraq to imperialist alliances, especially the Baghdad Alliance, and turned the country into a centre of conspiracy against the revolutionary movement of the Arab homeland. Thus, the 14th July Revolution was a historic event, but it soon suffered a set-back when it was dominated by the dictatorial rule of Abdul Karim Kassem. The Arab Ba'th Socialist Party therefore had to continue the struggle to restore the revolution to its genuine path.

THE ARAB BA'TH SOCIALIST PARTY

This Party under whose leadership Iraq is governed was founded on April 7, 1947. It had emerged in the early 1940's as a revolutionary, popular nationalist movement that struggles for the unity of the Arab nation, its freedom and socialism.

The Party's constitution emphasizes that the Arabs are one nation that has the natural right to live within one state, free to determine its own destiny. The Party's Regional Leadership is the highest party authority in each Arab country as is the case in Iraq, coming in party organization second to the Party's National Leadership, the highest party authority on the pan-Arab level.

The latter is responsible for party activity throughout the Arab countries.

8TH FEBRUARY 1963 REVOLUTION

On this day the Arab Ba'th Socialist Party carried out its great Revolution which brought down the dictatorial regime. It was a socialist, democratic and nationalist revolution in which all the civil and military formations of the Party took part, which elicited the hostility of imperialist forces. The latter combined in conspiring against it on 18th November, 1963, while it was only a few months old.

THE 17TH JULY 1968 REVOLUTION

The 17th July 1968 Revolution, under the leadership of the Arab Ba'th Socialist Party, is the most important event in the history of modern Iraq. A progresive Revolution, it succeeded in liberating Iraq from all forms of subservience, in rescuing the country's oil wealth from the control of international oil monopolies by the historic decision of Oil Nationalization of June 1st, 1972.

One of the great achievements of the 17th July Revolution is that it was able to close the ranks of the Iraqi people into a progressive, patriotic national front. It also promulgated the Law of Autonomy for the Kurds in Northern Iraq, on March 11th, 1974, and put it into practice, whereby autonomous legislative and executive offices were established, granted the minorities in Iraq their rights and brought peace and stability to the people.

On the pan-Arab level, the importance of the Palestine cause and its centrality in the national struggle was stressed. Working for the crystallization of the Arab masses' unity, supporting it economically, opening the doors of Iraq for Arabs to work and live, opposing the calls for a defeatist settlement, completely supporting the Palestinian Resistance and the Arab national movement, all were emphasized.

On the international level, the importance of the non-aligned movement and its support to gain leverage in the international community was affirmed. It is making an effective contribution in support of the peoples who are struggling to achieve their political and economic freedom; in addition, it supports liberation movements throughout the world, especially in the African continent,

South-East Asia and other Third World countries. The pan-Arab cause was regarded as the essential criterion in defining the form of relationship with any country whatsoever in the world.

PLANNING IN IRAQ

1. The Country's Development Plans:

The National Development Plan is based on the principles of the Arab Ba'th Socialist Party and the National Action Charter, in accordance with the Party's strategy, its phased programme, and its political and economic philosophy. Basically, the Plan aims at a balanced development, the stepping up of general and sectoral growth rates, and the attainment of higher national income rates which will secure a speedy increase of individual income, the raising of the standard of living and education, the general improvement of social services, and the effective provision of social security. It stresses the importance of new trends in planning methods and the intensifying of efforts for the speedy achievement of development objectives.

The National Development Plan therefore deals with the duties and functions of socialist building, the raising of living standards and the continuation of increase in individual purchasing power alongside better and more comprehensive services all around.

The Party has set a programme for revolutionary change in the country's conditions whereby it can become a firm base for Arab revolution and a model for a unified Arab socialist society. Hence the consolidation of the country's political independence by building up the State's revolutionary systems and the armed forces, the achievement of economic independence by the nationalization of monopolist oil companies, the creation of the National Progressive Front, the peaceful democratic solution of the Kurdish question and the implementation of the Autonomy Law, the founding of popular democratic practice by the formation of People's Councils and the support of mass organizations. Radical changes have been effected within the framework of socialist building: the socialist sector has been so expanded that it is now the leading sector in trade, industry, agriculture and basic social services. A Labour Law has been promulgated to secure the rights and interest of the working class, together with Pension and Social Security Laws which cover every employee in the State, whether civilian or military. Laws have also been passed to secure women's rights and their complete equality with men.

Iraq adopts five-year plans to absorb the financial revenues which have been on the increase ever since oil nationalization in 1972. The 1965—1969 plans were budgeted ID 621 million in all, but the 1970—75 plan alone was budgeted ID 2008 million, and the 1976—79 plan, ID 9952.6 million. The 1981— 85 plan attempts a balance between the various social sectors, but lends especial emphasis to rural development and takes into consideration general economic coordination and integration among Arab countries.

Iraq's national income in 1979 was ID 9792 million as against ID 850 million in 1969, thus showing an annual growth rate of 23.5 per cent. Wages and salaries have increased considerably compared to what they were before the Revolution, with special benefits going to workers and lower and limited income groups: minimum wages have risen by 122 per cent.

2. Investments:

Sums earmarked for the 1980 annual plan were ID 5240 million — which shows an increase by 176 per cent over the sums earmarked for all the plans together made before the 17th July 1968 Revolution, which points to the deep determination of the political leadership to bring about the radical transformation of the economic life of Iraqi society.

MINISTRY OF PLANNING

Ever since the first day of the 17th July Revolution the Arab Ba'th Socialist Party realized the importance of balanced scientific planning to channel the country's economic potentials and its people's capabilities. Five-year plans have been drawn, bearing in mind, on one hand, that the country's permanent wealth is agriculture and, on the other, that the industrial base is to be sufficiently widened to effect a balance with agricultural projects.

The socialist sector's contribution to national production went up from 24 per cent in 1968 to 84 per cent in 1980. For the same period, investments went up from 35 per cent to 80 per cent. Sums budgeted for the 1981 annual plan were ID 6743 m., which is 256 per cent of the total sums budgeted for all the plans made in twenty years before the Revolution.

The 1981 Plan aims at the development of productive capacities and the raising of growth rates within a balanced sectoral framework in order to effect the right change in favour of the agricultural and industrial sectors, and minimize dependence on oil.

In the industrial sector the Plan stresses the necessity of increasing the productivity of present means and the rate of their use, the expansion of industries dealing with basic needs, the trending towards heavy industry, and the further development of export industries that are dependent on local raw materials.

MINISTRY OF CULTURE AND INFORMATION

Laying special stress on information, the Arab Ba'th Socialist Party has tried hard in the last fourteen years to develop in palpable form the quantity and quality of all matters relating to culture and information in harmony with the principles of the Party and the Revolution and the continuous directives of President Saddam Hussein. A lot has been achieved which does the Ministry proud, but a lot is yet to be done. This is an indication of the continued growth and progress in the plans of the Ministry and its departments.

The 1981 Plan for the Ministry includes general and detailed guidelines for the best and most effective use of the media at home and abroad; they are to serve national interests and expedite development plans; to raise political awareness through national and socialist education; to spread the principles of the Party and the Revolution; to make them heard far and wide; and to publicize their achievements.

MINISTRY OF OIL

Oil Policy:

Ever since the first day of the 17th July 1968 Revolution, the Republic of Iraq has been pursuing an oil policy based upon national patriotic objectives.

All operations of foreign oil companies in the country were nationalized, whereby Iraq conducted a direct national exploitation of its oil wealth, placed oil revenues in the service of national development, increased refining capacity, began exploiting natural gas, founded the base of petrochemical industries and created a tanker fleet for Iraqi crude oil and a tanker fleet for oil products.

By deciding to nationalize the operations of the Iraq Petroleum Company in June 1972, Iraq simply aimed at securing its national sovereignty and possessing actual control of its oil resources. The decision had an immediate and far-reaching effect on the objective reality of oil and economic questions, locally and on the Arab and

27

international levels. It is this decision which created the historic change in international oil relations.

Iraq is one of the richest countries in oil reserves. It is also the sole country which markets its oil on a 100 per cent national basis to supply more than 50 countries. It started oil production on a direct national basis in North Rumaila oilfield in April, 1972. It is indeed one of the largest oilfields in the world in terms of oil reserves. Its production has been going up considerably, and it is entirely run by Iraqis. Within the plan drawn up for the oil sector the major oil projects have been built so far.

MINISTRY OF INDUSTRY AND MINERALS

The 17th July Revolution has spared no efforts in pulling the country out of its old retarded state by translating the concepts and principles of the Party into the creation of a new economy not based

MODERN FACTORY

solely on oil. The new economy has a diversity of resources for its productions whereby correlation becomes possible between the industrial sector, on the one hand, and the other sectors, on the other.

National Development Plans have always stressed the importance of maintaining industrial growth in order to create a material and technological basis for a socialist economy, with due balance between the agricultural and industrial sectors. Similarly, much care is given to the raising of the efficiency of the productive system and of production rates by technical and administrative development on all levels.

A variety of specialized industrial establishments have therefore been set up, all correlated in the light of comprehensive surveys of projects throughout the governorates. A multiplicity of training centres are busy training skilled workers and medium-grade staff by the hundreds.

Locally made goods have proved their worth in the competitive market vis-a-vis imported goods.

MINISTRY OF AGRICULTURE AND AGRARIAN REFORM

Agriculture has commanded especial interest in the thoughts of the Arab Ba'th Socialist Party both on the theoretical and the practical levels. It is regarded by the Party as a central question of great importance. The Party has a motto, "Agriculture is inexhaustible oil," and has therefore concentrated on improving it qualitatively and quantitatively. Much has been achieved as a result of this policy and more is to come.

In order to tackle the question comprehensively, it was essential that all production plans be reviewed in accordance with basic and practical rules, and scientific and socialist planning be introduced into agricultural activity. Annual conferences are held where plans are studied and discussed democratically. Sums earmarked for agricultural investment have been increased enormously after oil nationalization, so much so that the Ministry has been able to launch gigantic projects in fulfilment of its plans. They cover, among others, collective farms, chicken farms and cattle breeding.

In the 1980 annual plan ID 203,691,000 was budgeted for the Ministry and its various departments, whereas its budget for 1970—71 was a mere ID 6,364,000, and for 1974—75, ID 156,053,000.

MINISTRY OF TRANSPORT AND COMMUNICATIONS

This Ministry secures land, air and sea transport for men and goods, and undertakes all services in connection with cable and wireless communications and weather reports, together with the maintenance of all the facilities that perform these functions.

Land and river transport within the country is similarly served, whereupon modern road networks have been built to cover all the governorates, on the one hand, and to connect Iraq with the neighbouring countries, on the other. This sector has been the subject of intense development: the 1976—80 National Development Plan stresses that transport be fast and easy and of a high international standard. Transport and communications should be secured between production areas and marketing centres to ensure the rapid flow of goods and services in the country. Cable and wireless communications are to be provided even in the remotest parts, and efforts are made to make them available throughout the Arab homeland.

IRAQI AIRWAYS

PEOPLE'S INTERNATIONAL STADIUM

THE MINISTRY OF YOUTH

The youth of the country receive particular care from the Party's leadership, as they are the hope of the Arab nation in realizing its objectives.

In the last few years they have been prepared intellectually in accordance with the Party's directives. They are given every opportunity to improve themselves mentally and physically, which accounts for the fact that Youth and Scientific Education Centres and Sports Clubs are spread throughout the country, whereby young men are prepared for the tasks ahead in defending their homeland and achieving Arab national aims.

The Ministry of Youth is in charge of this. It was first started in 1967 under the name of the Ministry of Youth Care. It got its present name by a decision of the Revolution Command Council in 1969, and has been considerably expanded since then.

Baghdad

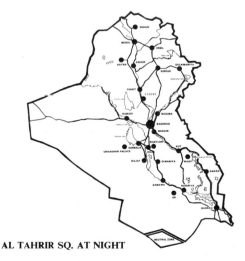

AL TAHRIR SQ. AT NIGHT

Dear Visitor,

In Iraq, all roads lead to the capital Baghdad, a city with a glorious past and a magnificent present.

It was built in A. D. 762 by Abbasid Caliph Abu Ja'far Al--Mansour on a site west of the Tigris. Famed for its circular plan, it was regarded as a model of city-planning, and soon became one of the great centres of human civilization.

The city spread out rapidly to the Eastern bank, reaching its peak in size and construction during the reign of Haroun Al-Rashid, in the latter part of the 8th century. For nearly five centuries it boasted palaces, public buildings, mosques, baths, markets, gardens, all of legendary renown.

After the 17th July Revolution, Baghdad has regained its ancient energy, making great strides in development, economy, education. With a population of over two million, its built-up area now covers more than 850 square kilometres, divided as it is by the Tigris into two halves, Rusafa and Karkh, which are connected by several modern bridges. In Rusafa is Rashid Street, the city's main street, stretching from North Gate to South Gate, and still very much the commercial centre of Baghdad, with the old souqs lined up on both sides. Parallel with it is the recently built Caliphs Street, where some historical mosques and churches, together with some new government offices, are to be found. In Sadoun Street stretching all the way from Liberation Square to Masbah, you will find most first-class hotels, cinemas, airline offices, travel agencies and some government departments, such as the State Organization for Tourism. Almost parallel with it is Abu Nuwas Street, a beautiful river-drive that runs by the Tigris from Jumhouriya Bridge to the 14th July Suspended Bridge.

In Karkh, the Western half of the city, is Damascus Street, stretching from Damascus Square to the International Airport Road, where you will find the International Railway Station, Zawra Park, and the vast grounds of the Baghdad International Fair.

Baghdad is a combination of all that is best in old and new. Multi-storey buildings often tower over ancient arcaded bazaars overflowing with fantastic things. A motley of colours, races, costumes, and ways of life gives the city an air of vitality and excitement. European dress rubs shoulder with Arab costume, blue jeans with ornate Kurdish clothes.

What to see in Baghdad

There is so much to see, so much you may want to take home with you, dear visitor. We'll try and help you a little. Of course, it all depends on how long you intend to stay.

BAZAARS

You want a souvenir of your visit to Iraq? Baghdad's famous souqs and bazaars have a vast variety of lovely oriental objects. You will find them mostly just off Rashid Street, between Martyrs (Shuhada) Bridge and Ahrar Bridge.

One of the most interesting is the Coppersmith Souq, where copper is still beaten in the old traditional way into pots and pitchers of all shapes and sizes. The noise is great and so is the sight. Shops spill over with copperware for household or decorative uses, to suit all tastes. Primitive, austere, elaborate, highly ornate — take your pick.

Further on you will come to one specialized souq after another in a labyrinth of arcades. Don't miss the Clothiers souq for a delightful sight of yards and yards of colourful material unfurled in

beautiful arrangements, or the Rugs souq where handwoven rugs in striking local motifs and colours are on magnificent display.

Nearby, on the other side of Rashid Street, is the so-called Shorjah, one of the most important trade centres of the city.

Chock-full of household wares, the place is aromatic with the smell of coffee, tea, spices and soap, and bustles with movement and noise.

Off Rashid Street again, along the river, is Mustansir Street, a woman's paradise for clothes, shoes, handbags, cosmetics. At one end of it you will find the traditional gold and silversmiths known for centuries for their lovely jewelry.

The are so many souvenirs and gifts which you can buy at the Folklore Centre, put up by the Ministry of Culture and Information

AL-BAZZAZEEN MARKET

in Sa'doun Street, near Karrada Junction, which has on display a tremendous variety of popular handicrafts from all parts of the country.

Within one month of their arrival, Iraqi nationals returning from travel abroad as well as foreign visitors can buy from the Duty-

POPULAR HANDICRAFTS

Free Shop in Sa'doun Street up to ID 60 worth of goods in foreign currencies.

There is another Free Shop in Sa'doun Street for members of diplomatic missions.

MUSEUMS

1. The Iraq Museum

Museum Square, Karkh.

Few countries in the world are as rich in archaeology as Iraq. The Iraq Museum, with its great well-organized and carefully labelled collection of archaeological finds is a reflection of this richness. A record of the many peoples and cultures which flourished in Mesopotamia from time immemorial up to the centuries of the Arab empire, the Museum offers a vivid display of pre-historic remains, of the civilizations and arts of the Sumerians, Akkadians, Babylonians, Assyrians, Chaldeans, Seleucids, Parthians, Sassanians, and Abbassids. The display halls are chronologically arranged in this order.

For the benefit of scholars, the Museum has a rich multilingual library, which adds to the prestige of the Iraq Museum as one of the best in the world of Mesopotamian studies.

Museum hours:
Winter: 9.00 a. m. — 5.00 p. m.
Summer: 9.00 a.m. — 1.00 p.m.
            4.00 p.m. — 7.00 p.m.

IRAQ MUSEUM

2. Museum of National Costumes and Folklore

Rashid Street, on the Eastern bank of the Tigris.

Apart from the peculiarly national character of the exhibits, the Museum's building is in an original Baghdadi style of architecture worth noting.

Museum hours: as above.

3. Museum of the Arab Ba'th Socialist Party

14th July Street.

It holds records of the Party's struggle ever since it was founded, including all the manifestos, statements, and studies published by the Party as well as records of the achievements of the 17th July 1968 Revolution.

4. The Baghdad Museum

Mamoun Street, near Shuhada (Martyrs) Bridge.

Traditional professions and popular customs of Baghdad represented in colourful life-size sculptures. Many of these professions and customs are fast disappearing but they are still very interesting to see, even as images. You will for instance see the old water-carrier, the weaver, the Zakariya Fast ritual, the bridegroom's ceremony, etc. A multilingual library on relevant subjects is also part of the museum. Paintings, photographs, maps and other illustrative material depict aspects of the city's history, together with the portraits of famous men who once ruled the city. It is administered by the capital's mayoralty. Open all days of the week.

THE WAR MUSEUM

OIL PAINTINGS ▶

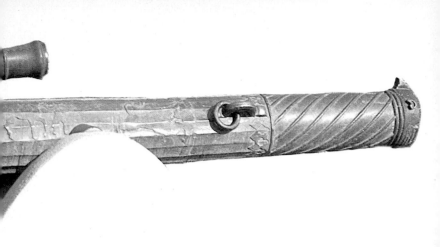

5. The War Museum

Adhamiya River-Drive, Kasra.

It exhibits many examples of old weaponry and a diversity of arms and military equipment used by the Iraqi Army since its foundation, showing the stages of its development. On display also are pictures of Iraq's revolutions and military achievements. Run by the Ministry of Defence.

6. National Museum of Modern Art

Kifah Street, near (Tayaran) Sab'awi Square.

It is a complex of four galleries, the largest of which is devoted to Iraqi modern art, with a permanent collection of paintings, sculptures and ceramics which is constantly being expanded.

Here the visitor can follow up the history of the Iraqi modern art movement from its earliest beginnings to the present. The other three galleries hold a large number of collective and one-man shows all the year round.

7. Museum of Iraqi Art Pioneers

It lies next door to the Museum of National Costumes and Folklore. Originally a house built in the old Baghdadi style in 1909, it holds the numerous works of over 20 artists whose paintings and drawings before 1949 laid the foundation of the modern Iraqi art movement.

8. Museum of Natural History

This Museum has grown into a Research Institute because its rich collection and library with more than 26000 books constitute an extraordinary basis for fundamental research.

PLACES OF SPECIAL HISTORICAL INTEREST

1. Mustansiriya School

The Mustansiriya School with courses in Arabic, Theology, Astronomy, Mathematics, Pharmacology and Medicine with application hospital, was the most prominent university in the Islamic world of Abassids.

It overlooks the Tigris from the Rusafa side, near Shuhada Bridge. It took six years to build in the reign of the 37th Abbasid Caliph Al-Mustansir Billah (A. D. 1226—1242), after whom it was called. Nearly three quarters of a million dinars in gold was spent on its construction and had an endowment valued at about one million dinars in gold from which the School obtained an annual revenue of 70,000 dinars to spend on staff and students.

It has a quasi-rectangular plan measuring 104.8 metres in length and 44.2 in width in the north, 48.8 in the south, making up an area of 4836 square metres. The built-up part totals 3121 square metres, the rest being a courtyard of 1710 sq. m. lined on all sides by *ewans* — large ornamented galleries completely open to the courtyard. There are rooms on two stories which were for students lodging, study and lecture halls, a library (which once held 80,000 books), a kitchen, a bathroom and, notably, a pharmacy attached to a hospital. It has its own garden, together with a house once specially used for the study of the Koran and another for the study of Holy Tradition.

MUSTANSIRIYA SCHOOL

THE GATE OF MUSTANSIRIYA SCHOOL

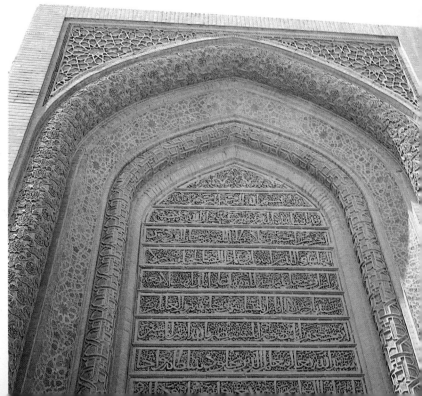

Mustansiriya was also famous for its clock which told the hours astronomically: apart from telling the hours, it specified the position of the sun and the moon at every hour, besides other mechanical curiosities.

2. Abbasid Palace

Near North Gate, on the river.

It is believed to have been built by the Caliph Al-Nasser Lidinillah (A.D. 1179—1225), in whose reign other notable institutions were built. It has a central courtyard and two stories of rooms, with beautiful arches and *muqarnases* in brickwork. It has a remarkable *ewan* with brickwork ceiling and façade. When it was partly reconstructed in recent times another *ewan* was built to face it. Because of the palace's resemblance in plan and structure to Mustansiriyah School, some scholars believe it is actually the Sharabiya School, mentioned by the old Arab historians.

Parts of the building were reconstructed by the State Establishment of Antiquities and Heritage, whereupon a collection of historical remains were exhibited in it representing certain stages of the country's Arab Islamic history.

ABBASID PALACE

KHAN MURJAN ▶

3. Murjaniya School

Known today as Murjan Mosque, this school is in Shorja, in Rashid Street. It was built by Aminuddin Murjan in 1357, that is, a century after the end of the Abbasids. In its early days it had rooms for students, like Mustansiriyah, but early in this century the school was pulled down, except for some parts, and replaced by a mosque.

4. Khan Murjan

Lying opposite the school, it was, together with other buildings and orchards, an endowment to help maintain the school and its scholars.

Architecturally, the Khan is extremely interesting. It is built round a great central hall with a high ceiling, with two stories of rooms on all sides looking on to it. To reach the upper rooms there is an elevated path built on brick-ornamented arches. Fourteen metres high and the only completely roofed Khan in Iraq, it is so roofed that light falls in from above from the apertures of the pointed arches.

It suffered neglect in later times until it was saved and reconstructed in 1935 and turned into a museum of Arab antiquities.

Today Khan Murjan is a first class restaurant where Iraqi dishes are served and folkloric music performed at night.

5. Baghdad's Walls and Gates

When Abu Jaafar Al-Mansour built Baghdad in A.D. 762, it was a round city, with walls and four gates at an angle of 90 degrees for defensive purposes. Main administrative and religious buildings were placed near the centre for easy approach. Although the capital was abandoned for Samarra in A. D. 836, the Abbasids went back to it in A. D. 892, and the city continued to expand on both sides of the river. Al-Mustarshid Billah, A. D. 1118—1135, was the first Caliph to build a wall on the eastern (Rusafa) side of the city, which remained until late in the 19th century.

The Eastern Wall was very thick, built from bricks, with several watch towers and a deep moat connected with the Tigris. The main gates were: Mu'adham (North) Gate, Dhafariya (Wastani) Gate, Halaba (Talisman) Gate, and Basaliya Gate.

AL-DHAFARIYA (WASTANI) GATE

The only gate extant today is the Wastani Gate, near the Tomb of Omar Sahrawardi — just off Sheikh Omar Street. It is a high cylinder-shaped tower with a ground circumference of 56 metres, 14.5 metres high, crowned with an octagonal dome. On the north-west side it has a portal 3 metres wide with a pointed arch, in front of which is a bridge across the moat. On the south-west side of the tower is a door that leads to an even bigger and higher bridge over the moat.

In the course of the extensive construction works undertaken by the government, workers on the speedy way near South Gate recently hit upon the remnants of what transpired to have been Halaba (Talisman) Gate, which was destroyed by the Ottomans in 1917. It had been last renewed some seven centuries earlier — in 1221; it has now been preserved with care, to stand as another monument telling a part of the history of Baghdad.

6. Tell Harmal (Shadoboum)

About 9 kilometres to the east of the capital, in New Baghdad.

One of the sites of ancient Mesopotamian civilization, dating back to Akkadian times and the Third Dynasty of Ur. Around 1850 B.C. the city became an administrative centre of the Ashnunna Kingdom. Large numbers of clay tablets were unearthed here, covering a variety of subjects, including the Ashnunna Laws, which preceded Hammurabi's Code by some two hundred years. The Science Academy here, the first in the world, was mainly concerned with mathematics. Tablets have been discovered bearing complex mathematical tables and theorems, including the so-called Euclid's theorem with its geometrical solution anticipating Euclid by about seventeen centuries.

TABLETS INSCRIBED WITH
MATHEMATICAL TEXTS, TELL
HARMAL/TELL DHIBAI (1800 B.C.)

An ancient city, some 30 kms. to the north-west of Baghdad, built on a Sumero-Babylonian plan in the 15th century B.C. by King Kurigalzu, on an elongated tongue of natural limestone. Water came to it from a large river (which branched out of the Euphrates) called by the Babylonian Bitty Inlil — the canal of the god Inlil, one of the greatest in the ancient Mesopotamian pantheon. The same river was called in Arab times Isa River.

The city's ziggurat, though partly ruined, commands the view with its 57 metres of height over the surrounding plain. Its base was 69 × 67 metres.

AGARGOUF ZIGGURAT

Only the lower level has survived, reinforced by an outer brick wall, with parts of the inner mud-brick core still protruding high above it. To hold the structure together matting and ropes were used every eight or nine rows, which also protected it from seepage and damp. The first story has three staircases in the middle, and two on the sides.

Other remains to see there are a number of palaces, temples and living quarters. Indications are that the city was inhabited right through the later Babylonian age and, in parts, even in Islamic times.

The State Organization for Tourism has put up on the site an information office and a rest-house with a large garden.

8. Ctesiphon (Al-Mada'in)

A historically important city on the east bank of the Tigris 30 kilometres to the south of Baghdad. It dates back originally to the 2nd century B.C. but amidst its extensive ruins stands a fabulous arch built in the middle of the 3rd century of our era. It is the largest single-span brick-built arch in the world: its construction at the time must have been a miracle of architectural planning. A descendant of ancient Mesopotamian structures in style, it embodied a skilful development of temples and palaces of the third millennium B.C., when the front part of great buildings would consist of large halls topped by high arches — as seen clearly at the entrances of Assyrian cities.

CTESIPHON (AL-MADA'IN)

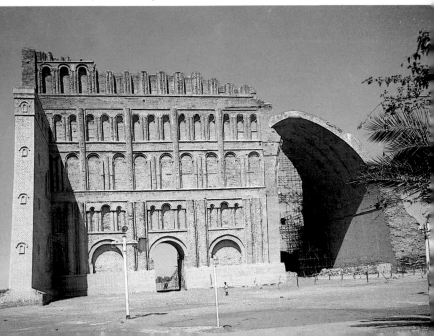

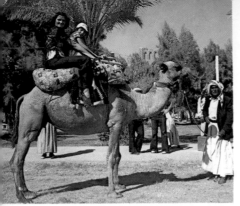

The *ewan* was the Arab extension of this style. In Arab Hatra the *ewan* type was well known. Excavations in the Temple of Allatu, built by Sanatruq I (A.D. 165—190) have shown that the Ctesiphon *ewan* was an exact copy of the Hatra original.

The arch is now 37 metres high, with a distance of 25.5 metres between the right and left hand walls, and 48 metres deep. The lower part of the walls is 7 metres thick.

Within a short walking distance there is a museum of local remains where detailed information is available. Open daily from 9.00 a.m. to 5.00 p.m.

In the town is also the shrine of Salman Al-Farisi, one of the Companions of the Prophet.

Apart from an Information Centre, S.O.F.T. has put up near the Arch a vast goat-hair tent in a green spot, furnished in Arab style with local hand-woven rugs and cushions, for visitors to rest and have a cup of coffee. It is an example of the kind of bedouin tent a visitor would be likely to see if he were to travel in the desert parts of the country.

Some distance away, overlooking the river, there is a tourist hotel together with a restaurant in the middle of an extensive garden. A tourist complex has been constructed nearby.

9. Qadissiya Panorama:

Dear Visitor,

While in Ctesiphon do not miss the Qadissiya Panorama, the most recent after the Panoramas of Moscow, Leningrad, Belgium and North Korea. It is a great sight, nationally and historically, a work achieved by the Iraqis in the days of the national liberation hero Saddam Hussein, in order to restore for all Arabs the glory of their past.

The Panorama is made up of consecutive scenes in which historical events are portrayed in graphic detail, aided with very striking light and sound effects. The historical events portrayed are those of the great battle of Qadissiya, which is here almost brought back to life with its din of warriors and clatter of arms and neighing of attacking horses.

QADISSIYA PANORAMA

The structure is based on old Iraqi ziggurats. It is 28 metres high, with an area of 2500 sq.m. The painting itself occupies a space 110 metres long and 15 metres wide — an area of 1640 sq.m.

SOFT has built nearby comfortable well-furnished apartments for visitors, with gardens, a cafeteria and a swimming pool.

*   *   *

SHRINES AND MOSQUES IN BAGHDAD

Wherever you go in Baghdad you will see domes and minarets ornamented in blue or glazed tiles, or covered with gold leaf. Many of them belong to shrines and mosques that have their stories to tell

KADHIMAIN SHRINE

about holy men who once rendered humanity great services with their teaching and their wisdom and piety. Their tombs, enshrined under these domes and minarets, have become places of worship and study and are visited by thousands of people every month. Here are some of them:

1. Kadhimain Shrine

A world famous shrine built in what used to be called in Abbasid times the Qureish Cemeteries. The two imams Musa al-Kadhim and Muhammad Al-Jawad are buried there. The great elaborate mosque, constructed in A.D. 1515, has two domes and four minarets all coated with gold.

2. Al-Imam Al-Adham Mosque

This mosque in Adhamiya was built over the shrine of Imam Abu Hanifa, who gave his name to the Hanafites. He was buried in Al-Khaizuran Cemeteries in A.D. 767, whereupon a small township grew up around the shrine called Mahallat Abi Hanifa. Three

AL-IMAM AL-ADHAM MOSQUE

hundred years later, in 1066, the Seljuk Sharaful Mulk Abu Said Al-Khuwarazmi renovated the shrine, built a large dome over it, and built a Hanafite school adjacent to it. The building went into cycles of change, destruction and reconstruction over the centuries, and was renovated by Ottoman sultans and walis several times. The Religious Endowments Ministry has recently expanded and renewed the whole mosque.

3. Sheikh Abdul Kader Al-Gailani Mosque

It is Sheikh Abdul Kader Al-Gailani's burial place, and the quarter where it was first built some seven centuries ago has been called after him, Bad Al-Sheikh (in Kifah Street) The shrine was

SHEIKH ABDUL KADER AL-GAILANI MOSQUE

originally a school built by Abu Said Al-Mubarak Bin Ali Al--Mukharrami, later improved and enlarged by his pupil Sheikh Abdul Kader Al-Gailani where he lived and contemplated and taught until his death in A.D. 1165. He was buried there. In later times the Ottoman Sultan Sulaiman the Magnificent constructed a high expansive dome over the holy man's tomb, together with many ancillary buildings.

4. Sheikh Omar Al-Sahrawardi's Shrine

In Sheikh Omar Street, near the Middle Gate (Al-Bab Al--Wastani).

This famous mystic and theologian died in A.D. 1225. The mosque over his shrine, one of the oldest extant in Baghdad, has a conical dome in Seljuk style.

SHEIKH OMAR AL-SAHRAWARDI'S SHRINE

5. Sitt Zumurrud Khatun's Tomb

On the west side of Baghdad, in Sheikh Ma'aruf district.

The tomb has a high octagonal "dome" in Seljuk style, one of the most remarkable in the city. Erroneously ascribed to Sitt Zubeida, wife of Haroun Al-Rashid, who was actually buried in the Qureish Cemeteries in Kadhimiya, it is in fact the tomb of Zumurrud Khatoun, wife of the Caliph Al-Mustadhi Bi-Amrillah, who had it constructed as a mausoleum for herself sometime before A.D. 1202, during the reign of her son, the Caliph Al-Nasir Li Dinillah.

SITT ZUMMURRUD KHATUN'S TOMB

6. The Caliphs Mosque

Half-way in Caliphs Street, near Shorja, is a new mosque with an ancient minaret that belonged to the Caliphs' Palace mosque about a thousand years ago. The latter mosque was built by Al-Muktafi Billah, A.D. 902—908, but the existing minaret was actually built much later, in 1289, on certain parts that pre-date it considerably. It is 33 metres high above ground level, with a base that has 12 sides measuring in all 20.64 m.

THE CALIPHS MOSQUE

14TH RAMADHAN MOSQUE AND THE OLD MONUMENT OF THE UNKNOWN SOLDIER

IBN BUNNIEH
MOSQUE

THE MARTYRS MOSQUE, IN UM ATTUBOUL

7. Other Mosques

There are several other old mosques in Baghdad known mostly for their domes and minarets, such as Sheikh Marouf Mosque and Khafafin Mosque. The latter was built by Zumurrud Khatoun.

There are also many recent mosques distinguished for their magnificent arabesques, glazed-tile walls and superb calligraphy, a characteristic of Islamic architecture, such as 14th Ramadhan Mosque, overlooking the Unknown Soldier's Tomb; the Martyrs Mosque, in Um Attuboul on the way to the International Airport; and Bunnieh Mosque, near the International Railway Station.

SOME OLD CHURCHES IN BAGHDAD

1. The Roman Catholic Church

Usually called the Latin Church.
In Caliphs' Street, near Shorja.

It was built in 1866 on the spot where the Carmelite Fathers in 1731 had built a small church named after the apostle St. Thomas. It is based on a cross plan with a great dome 32 metres high, and has many interesting statues and paintings. It was completed in 1871.

2. The Armenian Orthodox Church

Known as the Church of the Virgin Mary. Midan square, Rashid Street.

This is one of the oldest churches in Baghdad. It originally belonged to the Nestorians before its ownership was transferred to the Armenian Orthodox community. Especially interesting is its annual service in celebration of the Assumption of the Virgin.

THE ARMENIAN CHURCH

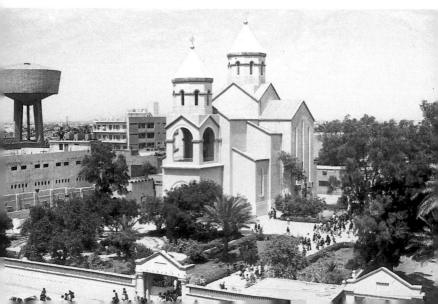

3. The Armenian Catholic Church

Souq Al-Ghazl, Caliphs' Street.

Begun in 1840 and completed in 1844. It was first called Church of the Saviour's Mother, then Church of the Assumption. In 1883 it was partly reconstructed and had its altar and doors renovated.

4. The Chaldean Church

Ras Al-Grayyeh, near Wathba Square.

One of the biggest churches of the turn of the century. Built in 1898 and called the Church of Mary Mother of Sorrows, it was later enlarged and had a cloister added to it.

5. The Syriac Catholic Church

Ras Al-Grayyeh, opposite Shorjah.

The first church to be built by the Syriac Catholics in 1841 and called Church of the Virgin Mary.

PLEASURE SPOTS
IN BAGHDAD

Extensive public gardens and outing spots are scattered throughout the city. Thousands of people go to them every day. The main ones are:

1. Abu Nuwas Street:

Stretching a long way by the great Tigris, between Jumhouriya Bridge and 14th July Suspended Bridge, the street was called after a famous Abbasid poet who was a daring bon vivant and a boon companion of the Caliph Haroun Al-Rashid, when Baghdad was at the peak of its glory. Further down, by the river-boats mooring place, there is a monument (by an Iraqi sculptor) of Shahrazad relating her Arabian Nights tales to king Shahrayar.

This street has ever remained reminiscent of our delightful poet: thousands of people every night crowd the cafes, bars and "casinos" that dot the river bank all the way down. Perhaps one of its loveliest sights is the series of little circular fires along the river on which mazgouf fish is grilled in an ancient way peculiar to Baghdad. A number of fishes are taken alive out of water, killed, gutted and transfixed on wooden pegs in a circle around a tamarisk wood fire. They are finally spiced and served with pickles and vegetables, a fabulous dish.

"AL-MAZGOUF" FISH AT ABU NUWAS STR.

ABU NUWAS STR. AT NIGHT

SUNSET AT ABU NUWAS STR.

ABU NUWAS
STREET

BAGHDAD HOTEL

2. River Trips:

You can go on trips up and down the Tigris by specially designed boats run by the State Organization for Tourism in accordance with a posted time-schedule. The trips start at the Boats Terminal half-way between the street that leads to the Unknown Soldier's Monument and 14th July Suspended Bridge.

At this Terminal S.O.F.T. has built an attractive restaurant with two dining halls, one for summer and the other for winter, surrounded by gardens all overlooking the river.

There are also private steam boats that undertake regular tours on the River. Their embarkation pier is in Abu Nuwas Street, by Jumhuriyah Bridge.

BOATS TERMINAL — ABU NUWAS STR.

3. Masbah Park:

Located in the district of Masbah by the Tigris River. It contains many statues of important Arab celebrities. It comprises some cafes and restaurants. It is famous for its old and tall trees.

4. Zawra Park:

Damascus Street.

A vast 1,200 donum park created by the mayoralty, extremely popular.

Special features: children's games, a zoo, exhibitions, a tourist's map, a summer theatre, an open-air cinema, sculptures and monuments, fountains, lakes, coffee-shops, restaurants, sandwich kiosks. Recently attached to it: the Zawra Olympic Swimming Pool.

In this green and watery spot the Zawra Tower has been built, 54 metres high, with a lovely Islamic dome. From the round veranda under the dome a panoramic view of much of Baghdad will be seen by the visitor, apart from the garden below, as though he were aflying over the city.

The top of the Tower is in three levels: one is for the 170 person cafeteria, the other, for the 135 person restaurant, and the highest one for the air-conditioning and cooling equipment. It has a lift with a capacity of 12 persons.

BAGHDAD TOWER — ZAWRA PARK

5. Luna Park

Army Canal Street.

The first of its kind in size and variety in the Middle East, it is a vast entertainment city created around a large artificial lake, where boats shaped like birds sail at leisure. A place for children, and grown-ups to spend many happy hours.

Coffee and ice-cream shops, restaurants, and sandwich kiosks are everywhere. Also a floating theatre.

6. Tajiyat Island:

A vast island in the middle of the Tigris near Fahama, north of Baghdad, has been turned by Amanat Al-Assima (Baghdad Municipality) into a veritable pleasure island, with all kinds of entertainment facilities, restaurants, swimming pools, children play-grounds, tennis courts, etc. There is a large artificial lake in it with a tower 60 metres high, from which the delightful views of the island can be

seen. The lake serves a sailing club and the visitors who may prefer rowing boats, as well as those who want to swim. There are also a night club, an open-air cinema, a multipurpose theatre, and a conference hall. Tajiyat Island is connected to the highway by three bridges, and it has its own network of roads.

500 donums in area, this beautiful spot has been completed at a cost of ID 30 million, and can cope with no less than 20,000 visitors a day.

Baghdad International Fair:

Damascus Street, at the entrance to Mansour.

This huge International Fair is held every year from 1st—14th October, when a large number of industrial countries and firms from all over the world meet in one great commercial event It also provi des and excellent opportunity to familiarise oneself with Iraq's progress in industry and agriculture. Entertainments of many kinds are available, including a Luna Park, apart from restaurants, casinos and refreshment kiosks.

BAGHDAD INTERNATIONAL FAIR

HOTELS, RESTAURANTS
AND TOURIST COMPLEXES

S.O.F.T.' hotels and restaurants in Baghdad are numerous and will be found in different parts of the city. Below is a list of the hotels, to be followed by a list of the major restaurants:

1. Mansour-Melia Hotel:

A 5-star hotel in Salhiya, overlooking the Tigris. It has 306 bedrooms, 620 beds, several suites, a conference room, restaurants and swimming pools. Its grounds have an area of 25 donums.

2. Babylon Hotel:

A large 15 story hotel in Jadiriya. It has 291 single and double bedrooms, 4 suites, a dining room, a hall for private parties, a reception hall, a cafeteria, a night club, etc.

3. Sheraton-Baghdad:

A 5-Star, 16 story hotel, off Abu Nuwas Street, overlooking the Tigris. It has a very large number of rooms, dining facilities, a night club, a sports club, conference and party halls, a cafeteria, a swimming pool, steam baths, beauty saloons.

4. Sadeer-Novotel:

A 5-star, 16 story hotel in Nidhal Street near Andalusia Square. It has 280 rooms, a restaurant, a conference hall. Total area: 20,220 sq. metres.

PALESTINE — MERIDIEN HOTEL

5. Palestine-Meridien:

A 5-star, 21 story hotel in Sa'doun Street, opposite the Sheraton. It has all the usual services, together with a bowling alley, a casino, tennis courts, swimming pools, mini-golf grounds, and gardens. Total area: 32,670 sq. metres.

6. Baghdad International:

A 5-star, 8 story hotel overlooking the Tigris.

It has 300 beds, bars, lounges, conference halls, postal services, a folklore shop.

7. Qadissiya:

A first-class hotel in Masbah, overlooking the Tigris. It has 250 beds. A project of the National Company for Tourist Investments.

8. Canal Hotel:

A first-class hotel in Army Canal Street.

It has 130 double rooms and 10 suites with all the usual facilities, including a night club and a swimming pool. Apart from being a commercial hotel, it is used for training hotel employees.

AL-CANAL HOTEL

9. Kadhimiya Hotel:

A first-class hotel in Kadhimiya, overlooking the Tigris. 250 beds.

10. Ctesiphon Tourist Complex:

It is in Ctesiphon 32 kms. away from Baghdad, overlooking the Tigris. It is one of the numerous complexes built by SOFT in order to make excellent tourist facilities available throughout the country. It has a first-class hotel, a restaurant, a bar, a swimming pool, a casino, together with 56 furnished apartments and 12 chalets.

CTESIPHON TOURIST COMPLEX

ABU NUWAS TOURIST COMPLEX

11. Abu Nuwas Tourist Complex:

It was built by S.O.F.T. in Abu Nuwas Island (once called Pigs Island) in the middle of the Tigris. It is made up of 40 furnished and air-conditioned apartments in groups of ten, each with bedroom, sitting room, kitchen and colour TV. The Complex has a large restaurant for inmates and visitors, and a big swimming pool. The woods around it have been turned into beautiful gardens, with places where 'mazgouf' fish can be cooked in the open air.

Tourist ferry boats carry visitors to it down the Tigris. They will find bands wating for them on arrival every Sunday and Thursday which play eastern and western music well into the night.

12. Ibn Firnas Hotel:

It is close to Baghdad's International Airport. It has 105 air-conditioned rooms each with colour TV and refrigerator. Swimming pool and other facilities as well.

Major Tourist Restaurants

A number of first-class restaurants have been recently built by S.O.F.T., where excellent food and drinks are served. They are:
1. Khan Murjan, in Samawal Street.
2. Candles (Shumu'), in Sa'doun Street (part of SOFT's building).
3. The Asian, in Jadiriya.
4. The Venice, in Jadiriya.
5. The Wharf (Marsa Al-Zawariq), in Abu Nuwas, on the river.

All these restaurants are extremely popular. Booking is advisable.

STATUES AND MONUMENTS
IN BAGHDAD

1. Statue of Sa'doun:

In Nasr Square, Sa'doun Street. Abdul Muhsin Al-Sa'doun was born in Nasiriya in 1889 and died in Baghdad in 1929. After World War I he became Minister of Justice and in 1922, Minister of Interior, after which he was Prime Minister four times.

In his fourth premiership he had some serious differences with the colonialists in Baghdad as a result of which he shot himself.

In 1933 the present statue, made by an Italian sculptor, was put up in honour of his memory.

2. The Unknown Soldier's Monument:

In Sa'doun Street. It was designed by Iraqi architects Abdulla Ihsan Kamel, Rifat Chadirji and Ihsan Shirzad and put up in 1959 in homage to all the soldiers who fell in defence of the country's dignity and pride.

THE UNKNOWN SOLDIER'S MONUMENT

3. Monument of Liberty:

In Liberation Square. It is the work of the late Iraqi artist Jewad Selim. One of the greatest works of art in the city, it depicts the struggle of the Iraqi people in the dark days before the 14th July 1958 Revolution for liberty, peace and prosperity.

It was unveiled in 1961.

MONUMENT OF LIBERTY

THE MOTHER

4. The Mother:

In Al-Umma Park. It was made by Iraqi sculptor Khalid Rahal in 1961 to represent the mother who is confident of her son's future now that the Revolution has given drive and hope to his generation.

5. 14th July Monument:

Near the Suspended Bridge. It was made by Iraqi artist Miran Al-Sa'di and unveiled in 1963. It portrays the courage and determination of Iraqi soldiers, four of whom are rushing forward to victory with a raised flag, while a fifth has fallen in battle.

6. Abu Ja'far Al-Mansour:

In Masbah Park. It was made by Iraqi sculptor Mohammad Ghani in 1968 to embody his idea of the second Abbasid Caliph (A.D. 713—775) who built Baghdad in A.D. 762.

7. Al-Kindi:

In Masbah Park. It was made by Iraqi artist Mohammad Al-Hassani in 1968 in memory of Abu Yousef Ishaq Al-Kindi, the great Arab philosopher, mathematician, doctor and musician, whose 300 books, whether original or translations, had a profound influence on Arabic thought.

8. Al-Mutanabbi:

This perhaps the greatest of all Arab poets, (A.D. 915—965) who was born in Kufa and lived in the desert and most of the great cities of his time, has two statues. One, in stone, in Masbah Park, was made in 1968 by Iraqi sculptor Abdul Rahman Gailani; the other, in bronze, in the National Library's courtyard, was made in 1978 by Mohammad Ghani.

9. Al-Razi:

In Masbah Park. It was made in 1968 by Saleh Al-Karaghoulli in memory of Abu Bakr Mohammad Zakaria Al-Razi, the great physician and philosopher of a thousand years ago, author, among 230 books, of the famous "Al-Hawi" (Comprehensive Medicine).

10. Al-Farahidi:

In Masbah Park, made by Miran al-Sa'di in 1968. Al-Khalil bin Ahmad Al-Farahidi (A.D. 718—786), a great linguist, philologist and grammarian, founded the science of Arab prosody and phonology. He wrote the first Arabic dictionary (one of the first in all languages) and also wrote essays on melody and rhythm.

11. The Eagles Monument:

In Eagles Square, made by Miran Al-Sa'di in 1969 in honour of the present generation which courageously seeks the fulfilment of the aspirations of the Arab revolution.

THE EAGLES MONUMENT

12. Al-Kadhimi:

In Kadhimi Square, made in 1972 by Iraqi artist Ismail Fattah. Abdul Muhsin Al-Kadhimi (1866—1935) was called Poet of the Arabs. He was one of the first intellectuals to call for Arab unity and independence, and his poetry for a long time inflamed the feelings of the masses in many parts of the Arab world.

13. Al-Rusafi:

In Mamoun Square, Rashid Street, made by Ismail Fattah in 1970. Ma'rouf Al-Rusafi (1877—1945) is one of the greatest Iraqi poets of modern times. Much of his poetry expressed a revolt against injustice and elicited great popular response.

14. Kahramana (Murjana):

In Ali Baba Square, made by Mohammad Ghani about the shrewd Murjana, Ali Baba's house-keeper (Kahramana), and the forty thieves. In the delightful Arabian Nights story, Murjana intelligently called off the ruse of the thieves hiding in forty big jars by pouring boiling oil on their heads one by one.

KAHRAMANA (MURJANA)

15. Hammurabi Obelisk:

In Qahtan Square, near Um Al-Tuboul Mosque, made by Saleh Al-Karaghoulli. The great Babylonian king and law-giver Hammurabi (1792—1750 B.C.) inscribed his famous code in an obelisk for his people to read it and act according to it. The original obelisk is now in the Louvre Museum.

HAMMURABI

16. Hammurabi:

In Haifa Street, made by Mohammad Ghani. The great Babylonian king Hammurabi founded the first extensive empire in Mesopotamia, and made laws for equity and justice which organized people's lives and soon became a model for legislation in many parts of the ancient world.

17. The Arab Woman:

In Zawra Park, made by Iraqi sculptor Nida Kadhim in 1971.

An Arab woman is offering a crown of flowers to the new generation intent on building a better future.

18. The Arab Horseman:

In Mansour Square, near Baghdad International Fair, made by Miran Al-Sa'di in 1972. The Arabs have always loved horsemanship and associated it with gallantry, courage and generosity — all the qualities that go into the making of a hero.

THE ARAB HORSEMAN

19. Abu Nuwas:

In Abu Nuwas Street, made by Ismail Fattah in 1962 — in fact, one of his best works. Al-Hassan Hani Abu Nuwas (A.D. 763—814) was a poet who lived in Basrah and Baghdad, a contemporary of Harun Al-Rashid and his son Al-Ameen. He glorified the easy ways of city life as against the harshness of bedouin life in delightful poetry of consummate artistry.

20. Shahrayar and Shahrazad:

In Abu Nuwas Street, near the Wharf, made by Mohammad Ghani in 1975. Shahrazad tells her one-thousand-and-one-night stories to king Shahrayar.

**SHAHRAYAR AND
SHAHRAZAD**

ABBAS BIN FIRNAS

21. Abbas bin Firnas:

On the way to Baghdad International Airport, made by Iraqi sculptor Badri Al-Samarra'i. Philosopher, poet and inventor, Abbas bin Firnas lived in Andalusia in the 9th century, in the reign of the Umayad Caliph Abdul Rahman II. He formulated his own theories about the possibility of human flight, in which he conducted experiments which earned him the name of the First Arab Flier.

22. Al-Wasiti:

In Zawra Park, made by Ismail Fattah in 1972. Yahya Al-Wasiti, painter and calligrapher, earned undying fame for his extraordinary illustrations of **Maqamat Al-Hariri** which he completed in 1223. An original manuscript is in the Bibliothèque Nationale, Paris.

23. Al-Farabi:

In Zawra Park, made by Ismail Fattah in 1965. Abu-Nasr Al-Farabi (A.D. 874—950) was one of the greatest philosophers of the Arab world, who wrote a large number of books on philosophy, logic, music and other subjects. He was called the Second Teacher — the First being Aristotle.

24. The New Unknown Soldier's Monument:

Near Zawra park, designed by Khaled Rahal, completed in 1982.

An embodiment of a complex architectural form, with much symbolism. A 550 ton shield is about to fall down, as the soldier falls, killed in battle, in defence of his country. Out of the middle of the monumental structure rises the Iraqi flag.

25. Monument of the March of the Leading Party:

In Museum Square, made by Khalid Rahal, and unveiled in 1980.

This large monument depicts the progress of the Iraqi people from time immemorial until the 17th July national socialist Revolution. It is in the shape of a giant ship emerging from red waves, the martyrs' blood. The sculptures interlock into an epic story of the early civilizations and their change over the centuries. Some of its figures are Gilgamesh, Ishtar, Buraq, together with a multiplicity of symbols leading up to the triumph of the peasant and, with the defeat of feudalism, his regaining of the land, to be followed by the striking achievements the Arab Ba'th Socialist Party has made possible for the Arab nation.

26. Fayek Hassan's Mural:

Erected in Younis Sab'awi Square in 1960, it was the first mural of its kind to be erected in Baghdad. It describes the people's desire to live in peace and their determination to continue the struggle that shall lead to complete independence, which is dearly guarded by all the sectors of the people.

27. The Monument of Abu Ja'far Al-Mansour:

In the Arab Quarter in Mansour, made by Khaled Rahal. It is the head of the Caliph on top of a tower reminiscent of the towers of the Round City's walls which he built twelve centuries ago. The tower, ornamented with arabesques, has inside it a small museum with an equestrian statue of Al-Mansour.

28. Oil Nationalization Mural:

On the road to the International Airport, designed by Iraqi artist Nizar Hindawi.

Standing 14 metres high and 12.6 metres wide, this is the largest mural in the Arab homeland. It sums up Iraq's history from Assyrian and Akkadian days up to the present, and shows the struggle and progress of the Party. It was put up in memory of the Decision to nationalize oil, whereby the country gained complete control over its petroleum wealth. On the other side of the mural are excerpts from the Decision's text.

THE NATIONAL THEATRE

The 1000-seat National Theatre in Fath Square is one of the most modern and best equipped in the Arab world. It has a 15 m. diametre revolving stage, and has two halls fitted for cinematic projection. Plays, concerts, musical evenings and film shows are regularly presented in it.

Diyala Governorate

Anbar Governorate

Habbaniya Tourist Village

TOURIST VILLAGE IN HABBANIYA

DIYALA GOVERNORATE

Situated to the east of Baghdad, it is one of the governorates of central Iraq, and is famed for its palm groves and fruit orchards, especially its citrus trees. Arab historians in the old days mentioned its innumerable trees and plentiful waters. The centre of the governorate is Baquba, some 66 kms. away from Baghdad.

This area is one of the more important in Iraq because of its ancient culture. Many archaeological tells have been identified, indicating early settlements that date back to the Al-Ubaid period, about six thousand years ago, the old Babylonian age, and the dawn of dynasties.

Our archaeological information here was derived from the excavations conducted before World War I. Further information

ALABASTER STATUE: ▶
SUMERIAN LADY — DIYALA
— TELL ASMAR 2600 B.C.

POTTERY JAR DECORATED
IN RED—DIYALA— TELL
AJRAB 2700 B.C.

has come to us from the more recent extensive excavations conducted at the start of the implementation of Himreen irrigation dam. The earlier digs revealed temples and palaces in ancient cities such as Tell Asmar (ancient Ishnunna), capital of the Ishnunna Kingdom, which flourished in the old Babylonian era. Also discovered here was the Khafaji site (ancient Tutoup), distinguished by its elliptical temple, about 15 kms. away from the old Diyala Bridge. Thousands of clay tablets and cylinder seals were found here, all belonging to the Babylonian period and the age of the dawn of dynasties.

Geographically and culturally important, the area kept its prominent position throughout the various Islamic eras.

Throughout the administrative centres of Diyala governorate you will find many privately owned hotels and casinos, together with tourist complexes, social clubs, excursion gardens, children's playgrounds, sports fields, modern markets, bookshops, public halls, cinemas and post offices.

ANBAR GOVERNORATE

Situated near Baghdad Governorate, it is in central Iraq. It used to be called Dulaim Liwa, after the famed Dulaim tribes which mostly lived in it, and later it was called Ramadi Liwa, after its main town, which is today the centre of the governorate. Ramadi itself is a comparatively recent city, built by the Ottoman Wali of Baghdad, Madhat Pasha (1869—1872). It is 105 kms. away from the capital.

The present name of the governorate belongs to the old historic town of Anbar, 5 kms. north of Falluja. Its antique ruins are still visible here and there, some of them surrounded by an old mud-brick wall.

Anbar flourished in pre-Islamic times. The historian Amianus Marcellinus referred to it in A.D. 363 as the second most important city in Iraq after Ctesiphon. It acquired special significance in Islamic times when the Arab General Sa'd bin Abi Waqqas built in it the third large mosque in Iraq and, later, when Abul Abbas al-Saffah, founder of the Abbasid dynasty, made it his capital in A.D. 752. Abu Ja'far Al-Mansour lived in it for some time before moving his capital to Hashimiya, near Kufa, and thence to Baghdad after he had built it.

Other major towns in Anbar governorate are Falluja, Heet, Haditha and Ana.

Falluja, some 60 kms. away from Baghdad, got its name most probably from an ancient site called in cuneiform tablets Pellugto.

Dear Visitor, having gone through Falluja, make sure you pay a visit to Habbaniya Lake and Tourist Village. You will find below a special section on it.

Beyond Ramadi you can visit the old city of Heet with its traditional water-wheels on the Euphrates. Heet was well-known in Sumerian, Babylonian and Assyrian times for being a main source of bitumen. There is an inscription in which the Assyrian king Tukulti

Ninurta (889—884 B.C.) says that he encamped near the bitumenous sources of Eed — meaning Heet.

Then off to Haditha, then to Ana to the north-west of it — another historic town which was once the centre of a region mentioned in Babylonian and Assyrian inscriptions. A most striking relic in it today is the unique octagonal minaret, which dates back in all likelihood to the eleventh century A.D.

A big project has been underway in Anbar governorate for some time recently: the Haditha Dam on the Euphrates for irrigation and electricity. Archaeological expeditions have therefore been conducting intensive search of many sites in the area and carrying away some important relics where they can be restored, before the area is flooded by the dam.

THE TOURIST VILLAGE IN HABBANIYA

It is the largest tourist village of the kind in the Middle East. 84 kms. to the west of Baghdad, off the road to Ramadi, it occupies an area of about one square kilometre, and stretches several hundred metres into the lake around which it has been built.

This tourist complex is made up of:

A 4-star 6-story hotel with a lounge, a conference hall, suitable also for film shows, 3 restaurants, bars, a summer and winter swimming pool, a library, a phlippers room, etc. Every floor has 47 double bedrooms and six suites (making up a total of 600 beds), all centrally air-conditioned with private bathrooms and colour TV sets. On the top floor there is a night club. 500 chalets, of which 300 have one double bedroom each, and the rest have two double bedrooms, with bathroom, kitchen, etc. all air-conditioned in summer and winter and attractively furnished.

Two large swimming pools for adults and children, two first-class restaurants, a lot of facilities for children's play, a youth club, a boating and sailing club, a horse-riding turf, 4 tennis courts, volleyball, archery, and mini-golf playgrounds, with a store for lending sports equipment. Also: a supermarket and an open-air theatre and cinema.

All kinds of other services are available in the Village: a pharmacy and dispensary, a nursery, hair-dressing salons, a post office, a bank, close-circuit TV, a spacious park for cars, etc. The beautiful Arab Tent casino is right on the lake, and gardens and lawns cover two-third of the whole area complete with a flower-and-plant nursery.

The Village has contributed much to the activitation of tourism within the country. Visitors from home and abroad go to it individually and in organised groups in large numbers, and many conferences are held in it periodically.

THE TOURIST VILLAGE IN HABBANIYA

THE TOURIST VILLAGE IN HABBANIYA

A Tour
in the South

You have now seen the most important sights of Baghdad and the nearby districts. Let us now take you southward. First, to Babylon.

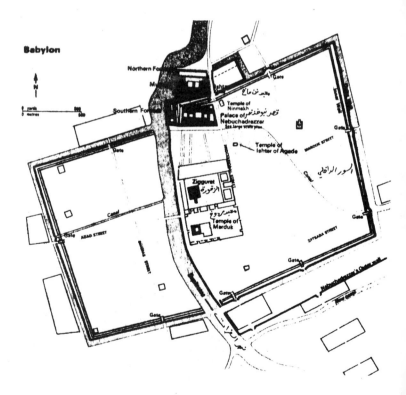

Babylon

N

Northern Fo

M

Southern Fo

Temple of
Ninmakh

Palace of
Nebuchadrezzar
See large scale plan

Temple of
Ishtar of Agade

Ziggurat

Temple of
Marduk

Gate

ADAD STREET

MARDUK STREET

ZATSABA STREET

Gate

Gate

Gate

Gate

Gate

Gate

Gate

Nebuchadrezzar's Outer wall

New Canal

Canal

**PLAN OF THE OLD INNER CITY OF BABYLON, WITH
THE WESTERN SUBURB, SHOWING THE PROCESSION STREET
AND PRINCIPAL BUILDINGS**

Babylon

Babylon lies 90 kilometres south of Baghdad, some 10 kilometres north of Hilla. The road to Babylon branches off the main Baghdad-Hilla highway.

A legendary city in ancient history Babylon figures prominently in the Bible as well as in the writings of travellers and historians for its wealth and magnificence. Its walls and Hanging Gardens were one of the seven wonders of the ancient world.

In Akkadian times, around 2350 B.C., Babylon was a small village which in five or six centuries had grown in size and importance, mostly during the reign of the Third Dynasty, until it became the capital of the famous king, law-giver and social reformer Hammurabi (1792—1750 B.C.). In the next thousand years or so it

**ISHTAR GATE AND THE STREET OF PROCESSIONS.
(RECONSTRUCTION)**

THE LION OF BABYLON

THE STREET OF PROCESSIONS

witnessed the growth of other Mesopotamian cities which surpassed it in power and influence until, in the 2nd Chaldean Kingdom (625—538 B. C.) it flourished again as the capital of a mighty and prosperous country. King Nebuchadnezzar (605—563 B. C.) rebuilt it in accordance with a new plan that took especial care of its fortifications, and Babylon thus became the largest and loveliest city of its time.

THE GREEK THEATRE — BABYLON

As he was pursuing his conquests, Alexander the Great stopped for a time in Babylon. He later returned only to die in it in 322 B. C. Seleucus, one of his commanders and successors, built Seleucia, south of Baghdad, whereupon Babylon lost its political significance.

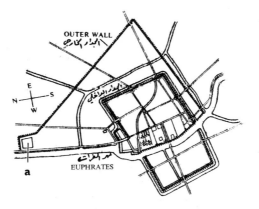

BABYLON AT THE TIME OF NEBUCHADNEZZAR II (605—562 B.C.) WITH FORTIFICATIONS EXTENDED TO ENCLOSE THE SUMMER PALACE (a) IN THE NORTH

THE TEMPLE OF NIN MAKH

Penetrated by the Euphrates from north to south, Babylon was surrounded by a moat and a double wall: the outer wall was 16 kms long, the inner, 8 kms. Straight, wide streets intercrossed, all paved with bricks and bitumen. The most important was the Street of Processions, which passed through Ishtar's Gate and ended in the Stepped Tower. The remains of this street with its bituminous paving are still there to be seen today.

THE LOWER PART OF ISHTAR GATE — BABYLON

Nebuchadnezzar's Southern Palace (190 × 300 metres) is situated on the west side of this major street, made up of five courtyards each surrounded by halls and a diversity of chambers, one of which is the throne room, 52 × 25 metres. The Hanging Gardens, the remains of which are still visible, were part of this palace.

NEBUCHADNEZZAR'S SOUTHERN PALACE

To the east of the Street of Processions lies Nin Makh's Temple, now reconstructed. To the north are the remains of the Main Palace, where the Lion of Babylon is. It should be noted that many remains lie under the accumulations of later buildings, as the place continued to be inhabited, or have been so submerged by the Euphrates that it is almost impossible to retrieve them.

On the way to Babylon, on the right-hand side, is the amphitheatre which dates back to the time of Alexander the Great, who for some years made Babylon the capital of his empire.

The Ishtar Gate, in a depression a little short way off the Street of Processions, still has some of its old wall decorations of bulls, symbol of Adad, god of storms, and dragons, symbol of Marduk, the chief god. The dragon here is a composite animal with the physical attributes of snake, lion and eagle. These brick reliefs are not glazed, as the beautiful glazed-brick panels figuring bulls, and dragons and lions (symbol of Ishtar) which decorated the Gate, the Palace and the Street of Processions were all taken, prior to World War I, to Berlin by the German expedition which excavated Babylon then. Along the Street, on the left a brick column is seen, which may have had a statue standing on it.

The Lion of Babylon, carved in basalt, reminds us again that the lion was the symbol of the goddess Ishtar. In the sculpture, the lion's back has marks indicating that it was meant for a precious saddle upon which Ishtar would stand.

To the south of the Street of Processions is a major temple, the Esagila ("the lofty house"), leading on to the site of the stepped Tower of Babylon, which had seven levels rising to a height of 91 metres, on a square base also 91 metres square. The Street runs straight until the bridge across the Euphrates, which rested on bastions 9 metres thick each.

Another temple in the area is Nabushcari, recently dug up with painted murals, the largest temple of its time.

As you cross the railway line to the city, you will see a rise which originally was 18 metres high with a palace built on it, which archaeologists call the summer palace of Nebuchadnezzar. In the upper parts of the back walls are ventilation apertures which served the inner rooms and halls of the palace.

The Revolution government has shown especial interest in Babylon. In 1978, it adopted a project for its revival and intensive excavation has since made many new discoveries, such as the southern part of the Street of Processions adjacent to the Tower's sacred wall, and many dwelling-places in the Ishtar Temple quarter and other spots. A number of buildings have been reconstructed, such as parts of the Ishtar Gate, the Southern Palace of Nebuchadnezzar, the temples of Ishtar and Nabushcari, the Greek amphitheatre, and some model Babylonian houses.

For visitors' convenience, S.O.F.T. has built nearby tourist apartments, a restaurant and a coffee-shop, and provided gardens and a car park.

In Hilla, on the river-front, the National Tourist Investment Company has constructed a tourist "casino" in the middle of a vast garden 15,000 square metres in area.

The City of Kish (Al-Uhaimir)

When you have crossed the railway line on your way to Babylon, you will find on the left a sign pointing to a site which once had its importance in ancient Iraq. It is Kish, or Al-Uhaimir ("the red" because of its ziggurat's red bricks); a well-built secondary road

**MARBLE VASE. KISH
2500 B.C.**

will lead you to it. It is specially significant because ancient Iraqis believed that kingship, after the Flood, descended from heaven again to Kish, and not as previously to Eridu near Ur. In this city lived the magnificent Akkadian King Sargon, founder of the very first empire in history.

You will find standing in front of you the remains of the city's red ziggurat on a rectangular base measuring 190 × 180 ft. On the other side of the city there once stood two more ziggurats and a temple, still partly extant.

Borsippa

When you leave Babylon for Kufa you will see a long distance away on the right the ruins of a unique city, 15 kms. to the south of Babylon: Borsippa, or Birs Nimrud. It had its own religious significance as the place for the worship of Nabu, son of the great Babylonian god Marduk. You can still see the 47 metre high structure which was once its seven-level ziggurat. If you climb it, you will wonder what those dark-green lumps of molten bricks are. Some scholars believe that the tower was one day hit by a comet which melted its bricks.

From the top, looking at the green country around you, you will see the traces of excavations that date back to 1902, as well as the temple of Nabu, Esida ("the firm house") and a prayer mosque.

Kerbala

It lies 102 kms. away from Baghdad, 78 kms. away from Najaf and 45 kms. away from Hilla. It witnessed great events which left their mark on Islamic history — mainly the tragic Battle of Tuff, in which were martyred Imam Hussein bin Ali and his brother Abbas together with many others, who are buried in their two great shrines in the city. Kerbala, though practically on the edge of the desert, lies amidst fruitful orchards thick with greenery and palm trees. Its streets and markets are always crowded with visitors and pilgrims.

The city has the 250 room Howra Hotel, built by S.O.F.T., as well as the 250 room Kerbala Tourist Hotel.

50 kms. away, in the desert, is the famed Ukhaidher Castle.

IMAM AL-HUSSEIN SHRINE — KERBALA

**ABU AL-FADHIL
AL-ABBASS
SHRINE —
KERBALA**

105

IMAM AL-HUSSEIN SHRINE

GATE OF THE SHRINE OF IMAM AL-HUSSEIN — KERBALA ▶

Ukhaidher Castle

Castle or palace, Ukhaidher is certainly one of the greatest monuments of early Islam you can see in this area.

It was built by the Arabs with stone and plaster on a plan which suggests the high skill of its architects in the use of vaults and arches. Most scholars believe that it goes back to the eighth century — that is, the beginning of the Abbasid age.

50 kms. away to the south-west of Kerbala, this has always been the most prominent structure on the way between Iraq and the Upper Euphrates and Syria.

A fortified wall runs round the palace, exactly like a warlike castle. Its rectangular measurements are 175.8 × 163.6 metres, with a height of nearly 21 metres. In the middle of each side is a large tower which also acts an entrance to the castle. The inner residential part is at some distance from the wall, except on the northern side. An annex was added to the middle of the eastern wall, and another in front of the western wall.

UKHAIDHER CASTLE

The main parts are a guards room, reception halls, dwelling apartments, a mosque and a bath. All these are gathered in one rectangular combine measuring 112 × 80 metres.

The castle has been the subject of great interest to the government, which has a special project for its maintenance. For visitors' comfort S.O.F.T. has turned a small part of it into a rest--house cum restaurant.

Ain Al-Tamr

Not very far away are the remains of the historical city of Ain Al-Tamr (Shuthatha). Although its first settlements date back to the pre-Christian era, it flourished in the 2nd and 3rd centuries of our era, and acquired particular importance after the Arab conquest when it became a major military and trade centre and was the birthplace of a number of famous men, notably Musa Ibn Nusair,

the Arab general who conquered Spain and became the ruler of Seville.

Today Ain Al-Tamr is the largest oasis in the Western plateau, famed for its palm groves and fruit orchards and lovely scenery. Its pleasant climate in Spring and Autumn, together with its mineral waters (from no less than 50 natural springs), makes it a very attractive spot to visitors. A Rest-House, a restaurant and a number of chalets have been built in the area by the State Organisation for Tourism.

Razzazeh Lake

On the way to Ukhaidher, some 18 kms. from Kerbala, is Razzazeh Lake, 60 × 30 kms. In recent years this beatiful large lake has been drawing lovers of swimming, water sports and fishing in great numbers. The Government has put up in the region many touristic facilities, afforested and planted extensive areas, and made arrangements to have the place supplied with purified water and electricity.

RAZZAZEH LAKE

THE SHRINE OF THE IMAM ALI IBN ABI TALIB — NAJAF

Najaf

Just 8 kms. away (and 60 kms. to the south of Hilla) is the holy city of Najaf, where lies the Shrine of the Imam Ali Ibn Abi Talib with its resplendent golden dome and minarets. Great quantities of

QASHANI IN THE SHRINE OF THE IMAM ALI IBN ABI TALIB — NAJAF

priceless objects, gifts of potentates and sultans, are treasured in the mosque. One of Islam's most important seats of religious instruction, Najaf has many schools where grammar, theology, history and literature are taught. Thousands of pilgrims visit the city annually.

A Tourist 250 room Hotel has been put up in it by the State Organization for Tourism.

Kufa

An important Islamic town of early Arab history, Kufa was the first Arab capital proper, founded by Saad bin Abi Waqqas in A. D. 618 and adopted by Ali bin Abi Talib as the centre of his caliphate. It had four sectors with the House of the Caliphate and the Mosque occupying the central space.

Its main mosque with the golden dome holds the tombs of Muslim bin Aqeel and Hani bin Arwa. It stands on the site of the original first mosque which excavations have shown to have been, square in dimensions. It has 28 semi-circular towers.

Next to the mosque and the house of Imam Ali is the reconstructed House of the Caliphate ("Dar Al-Imara"), which has an outer square wall, each side 170 metres long, 4 metres thick, with 6 semi-circular towers supporting each side, with the exception of the northern side which has only two towers. The inner building is also squar-shaped, 110 metres to every side with walls two metres thick, and similarly supported by semi-circular towers. It has a number of halls, *ewans* and courtyards.

Nippur

It lies 35 kms. to the north-east of Diwaniya, 180 kms. to the south-west of Baghdad.

Nippur has yielded us a large number of antiquities that span the Sumerian and Babylonian periods, up to Abbasid times. It was a large city, neatly divided by old Euphrates. On the east was the temple area, which held the ziggurat and the temple of Inlil, god of the wind and creator of the universe. Outside its walls is the "tell of tablets" where excavators have dug up an enormous number of tablets containing all kinds of knowledge.

The square ziggurat, 15 metres high, had probably several levels with three stair-cases, like other Mesopotamian ziggurats, all built of mud-bricks enveloped with hard bricks. It dates back to the time of king Ur-Nammu (see 'Ur').

STATUE FROM NIPPUR

Sawa Lake

Located near Samawa, in Al Muthanna Governorate, Lake Sawa is famous for its natural beauty. A nearby Rest House and Restaurant cater for the visitors to the Lake.

Uruk (Warka)

One of the most famous Sumerian cities of ancient Iraq. It was continuously inhabited from about 4000 B. C. up to the 5th century A. D. Because of the part it played in Iraqi culture for such a long time you may want to spend some time among its ruins.

Uruk lies about 30 kms. to the east of Samawa, and in the past it used to be on the Euphrates before it changed its course so much that it is nearly 12 kms. away. It was an important city on two scores: religion and science, which is confirmed by the thousands of clay tablets dug up in it which go back to the beginnings of writing — about 5000 years ago — in the invention of which Uruk played a major role. It was also the centre of the worship of the goddess

◀ VOTIVE VASE — WARKA
3000 B.C.

▲
GOLDEN DIADEM. WARKA
300 B.C.

Inanna, or Ishtar, which is symbolized by the star Venus. Her worship went to the Greeks and Romans under the name of Aphrodite or Venus, who had exactly the same attributes as Ishtar.

Uruk was renowned for its walls which cuneiform texts say were first built 4700 years ago by the Sumerian King Gilgamesh, hero of the epic named after him. The city limits and traces of its round walls are visible today. The latter are about 9.5 kms. long.

Among major remains is the ziggurat of Inanna—Ishtar which rises to a height of 16 metres on a square base measuring 60×60 metres. It dates back to the time of Ur-Nammu, 4000 years ago. In its neighbourhood are the ruins of a temple which used for mural ornamentation thousands of coloured clay cones.

Another temple in ruins is the one devoted to Anu, god of the sky, built with mud brick some 5000 years ago. Nearby is another temple devoted to Anu and his wife Anu-Antim, but it is a comparatively recent structure: it was built in Seleucid times, about 2,200 years ago.

An even more recent structure is the brick temple whose facade is ornamented with arches and columns, together with decorative brickwork of animals and geometrical patterns. It was built around A. D. 110.

The City of Ur

Excavations have proved that Ur was leading among the old Sumerian cities of Mesopotamia. Its earliest dwellings go back some six-thousand years, and after it had enjoyed prominence in the dawn of dynasties, 4800—4300 years ago, it assumed a leading position during the Third Dynasty of Ur, over 4000 years ago. In later times, although political leadership shifted to other Babylonian and Assyrian centres, it maintained its importance and kings continued to lavish their care on its temples and institutions.

The landmarks of the city lie within a large area the inhabited section of which measured 1200×700 metres. It was encircled by a mud-brick wall, almost elliptical in shape. The most important structure was the holy pyramid, which contained all the major temples together with the magnificent 3-level ziggurat built by Ur-

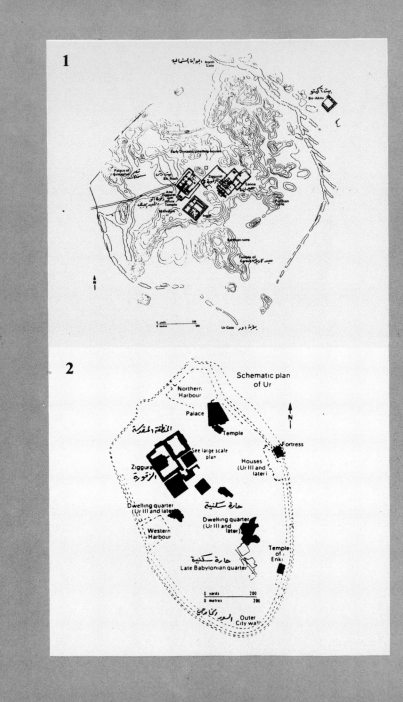

1

بوابة الشمالية North Gate

بيت أكيتو Bit-Akitu

Early Dynastic dwelling houses

Palace of Enmahgal قصر إنمهجال

Ziggurat الزقورة

E-Nun-Mah

Am Zigurat the Wing and Other Temples

Ehursag

Enunmah أننمخ

Nabonidus

Giparu

Harbour

Babylon ruins

Temple of Ganuch معبد كانونه

N

0 yards 500
0 metres 500

بوابة أور Ur Gate

2

Schematic plan
of Ur

Northern
Harbour

Palace

Temple

Fortress

المنطقة المقدسة

See large scale
plan

Houses
(Ur III and
later)

Ziggurat الزقورة

Dwelling quarter
(Ur III and later)

حارة سكنية

Dwelling quarter
(Ur III and
later)

Western
Harbour

Temple
of Enki

حارة سكنية
Late Babylonian quarter

N

0 yards 200
0 metres 200

السور الخارجي
Outer
City wall

3

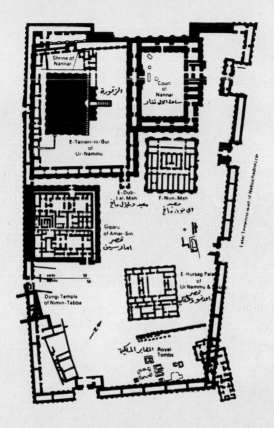

Shrine of Nannar

الزقورة

Court of Nannar
ساحة الاله ننار

E-Temen-ni-Gur of Ur-Nammu

Later Temenos wall of Nebuchadnezzar

E-Dub-lal-Mah
معبد دبلال ماخ

F-Nun-Mah
معبد نو نماخ

Gipar-u of Amar-Sin
قصر اماسين

yards
50

metres
50

Dungi Temple of Nimin-Tabba

E-Hursag Palace of Ur-Nammu & Dungi
قصر اورنمو ودنكي

Royal Tombs
المقابر الملكية

1. SITE-PLAN OF THE CITY OF URUK/WARKA, SHOWING THE ANU AND EANNA PRECINCTS IN WHICH PROTOLITERATE TEMPLES WERE FOUND

2. THE CITY OF UR AT THE TIME OF ITS THIRD DYNASTY AND LATER. URNAMMU'S CITY-WALL WAS DESTROYED BY THE ELAMITES IN 2006 B.C.

3. THE GREAT TEMENOS OR SACRED ENCLOSURE AT UR DATING FROM THE TIME OF THE THIRD DYNASTY (2113—2006 B.C.), SHOWING SOME LATER FEATURES.

UR ZIGGURAT

Nammu, founder of the Third Dynasty of Ur (2124—2107 B.C.) The lower level measures 62.5 × 43 metres, the third, 20 × 11 metres. The whole structure was 17.25 metres high.

The favourite god of Ur was Sin, or Nannar, the moon-god. His ground temple was built near the ziggurat.

Another prominent building was the palace of king Shulgi, son of Ur-Nammu, situated in the southern corner of the sacred area. Of a square plan, 55 × 55 metres, it used to be called the Mountain House.

UR ZIGGURAT
(RECONSTRUCTION)

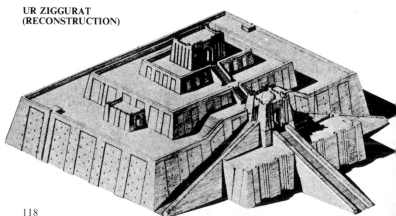

To the east of the temple area is a huge pit which was a vast cemetery dating back to the third dawn of dynasties, 4500 years ago. It contained about two-thousand graves which have yielded a veritable treasure of rare objects that have enriched the display halls of many museums, such as the Iraq Museum in Baghdad, the Nasiriya Museum, the British Museum, Pennsylvania Museum, etc.

DECORATED STONE BOWL FROM UR (3000 B.C.)

These objects range from musical instruments (e. g. the "lyre of Ur") to gold and silver ornaments and precious jewellery. Next to it is the cemetery of the kings and princes of the Third Dynasty of Ur. Its special feature is its sloping roofs. Not far away one can roam at leisure in a once-inhabited quarter that dates back to the old Babylonian era.

A rest house has been built in Nasiriya, about 15 kms. from Ur archaeological site.

GOLDEN HELMET
OF KING MES-
-KALAM-DUG.
UR 2450 B.C.

GOLDEN HARP
FROM UR

Wasit

Dear Visitor, as you tour the south, perhaps before going to the fantastic world of the Marshes, it would be a good thing to go to Wasit governorate. 65 kms. away from the governorate's centre Kut, lies the ancient city of Wasit amidst its ruins. It was built on a once vital spot by Al-Hajjaj bin Yousef al-Thaqafi, the governor who was sent to run the affairs of Iraq by the Omayyad Caliph Abdul Malik bin Marwan, around A. D. 702. It took three years to build.

KUT DAM — WASIT

It was divided in two parts by the Tigris, although the eastern part pre-dated the western. Wasit in Arabic means "in the middle" — as the town half-way between Kufa and Basrah. It had a number of large buildings, such as its mosque, and its imposing palace known as the Green Dome. Apart from the palace and the mosque, Al-Hajjaj also built an extensive souq.

Four stages in the building of its main mosque have been identified by the archaeologists: the earliest going back to the time of Al-Hajjaj which is a quadrangle surrounded by ornamented arcades resting on large sand-stone columns. The latest stage goes back to the Ilkhanid period of the 14th century.

Your attention will be caught by a structure at whose entrance rise a couple of beautiful brick-built minarets. It is rectangular in

121

shape, 52 × 24 metres, enclosing a tomb in a square room. Many generations after the city had been built the Tigris changed its course gradually, which might explain why the city was almost completely abandoned by the 17th century.

There are many archaeological tells in the area, such as Tell Na'man and Najma, some 60 kms. away, Tell Waldiya and Tell Sabis which lies 15 kms. away to the south-east of Kut. The last dates back to early Islamic times.

The Marshes

And now, off to a unique world, the Marshes, where nature seems to preserve its virgin aspect. Miles and miles of water, with an endless variety of birds, of fish, of plants and reeds and bullrushes, dotted as far as the eye can see with huts, each a little island unto itself, with slender mash-houfs shuttling back and forth through the reeds and flowers. This vast expanse of water is shared by three

FISHING IN THE MARSHES

THE MARSHES

◀ A MARSHES HOUSE FROM
THE INSIDE

southern governorates: Thi Qar, Misan and Basrah. Old Arabic books suggest that the Marshes were the aftermath of a devastating flood which took place around A.D. 620, but archaeological indications suggest that they were formed long before Sumerian times, when the Arabian Gulf waters began to recede southwards, leaving behind all those marshes alongside the Tigris and Euphrates.

The best months for taking trips in the Marshes are March and April. The weather then is pleasant, and the whole place is shot through with plants and flowers. Reeds may rise 20 feet high and papyrus, 10 feet.

In the winter season water birds of all kinds migrate to the Marshes, which then becomes a hunter's paradise. Fish, however, are always plentiful and the local inhabitants catch them with nets or spear them with a five-pronged 'fala', peculiar to the area.

People in the Marshes live in huts built from reeds and reed-mattings, with attractive designs that go back to ancient times. They look like hundreds of islands clustered together into small townships. Most prominent among them is Chebayish, on the left bank of Euphrates. Each "island" is in fact a man-made mixture of earth and papyrus pressed hard (to form a base of a hut) and called "chebasheh". The watery "streets" are plied by boats of different kinds and sizes, the most popular being the mash-houf, which is made from reeds and bitumen.

A delightful scene is a Marsh wedding, when the bride is carried in a lovely "regatta" made up of her own mash-houf and those of her party, all loud with men's lilting songs and women's joyous cries.

In recent years, schools and dispensaries have been put up on every spot in the area, however far or inaccessible.

The State Organization for Tourism has built a number of tourist cabins in Chebayish, in a slightly elevated place surrounded with palm groves and orchards. The cabins, looking rather like a bedouin encampment, have a brick-built interior with a papyrus exterior, each made up of one bedroom, kitchen and bathroom, all well-furnished. A tourist complex is being planned for this attractive area.

To get to the Marshes there are two ways: 1) by car from Nasiriya to Chebayish (a distance of about 100 kms), and thence by boat to tour the place; 2) by car from Basrah to Qurna (a distance of 74 kms), and thence by motor-boat to the Marshes, or by car again for another 45 kms.

Basrah

Basrah was the starting-point of Sindbad the Sailor's adventurous voyages to the world. When you see it today you will be reminded of the commercial importance it has enjoyed for centuries: endless ships shuttle back forth on Shatt-Al-Arab, on which it is built. It is Iraq's Port on the Arabian Gulf. All around it are millions of palm trees whose delicious dates belong, literally, to hundreds of categories.

AL-SHANASHEEL IN BASRAH (TRADITIONAL ARCHITECTURE)

CANALS AND PALM GROVES IN BASRAH

Basrah was founded by Utba bin Ghazwan on orders from Caliph Omar bin Khattab in A. D. 637, and has been a major Islamic city ever since. It started by being an administrative centre and in less than forty years it had a population of 300,000. Its golden age was under the Abbasids when, together with its suburb Ibilla, it became the focal point of Arab sea trade which went as far as China.

Even more significantly, Basrah was in those days an intellectual centre of the first order, with its great mosques and libraries, where many philosophers, scientists and grammarians flourished. One might mention such luminaries as Hassan Al-Basri, Al-Farahidi, Ibn Serene, Al-Asma'i, Al-Hariri — as well as Ibn Al-Jowzi and Ibn Al-Haitham (whose discoveries in optics and mechanics taught Europe a great deal). The city now has a museum which tells the story of this magnificent past.

The Revolution government has earmarked large sums of money for the unearthing and reconstruction of a large number of Basrah's ancient historic buildings, in an attempt to revive the city's great heritage. S.O.F.T. is contributing a great deal in this respect.

Basrah is 67 kms. to the north of the Arabian Gulf, 50 kms. away from the Iraq-Kuwait border, and 549 kms. to the south of

PALM TREES AT SUNSET

HOUSES IN BASRAH

Baghdad. It is connected with Baghdad by very good roads and regular air routes. It is also connected with Baghdad by railway. It is Iraq's outlet to the sea — to the Arabian Gulf States and the Far East.

SHATT AL-ARAB

Today Basrah is a large city criss-crossed with streets, waterways and canals, hence the rubric "Venice of the East", with public gardens everywhere. Its old architecture is Islamic in style, its new buildings modern in spirit. The city is made up of three main residential areas: Basrah proper, Margil and Ashar, the last particularly interesting for the curiosities that fill its bazaars.

Places of arhaeological interest: the old town originally built by Utba bin Ghazwan in the reign of Omar bin Al-Khattab; Imam Ali's Mosque, built in the year 14 after the Prophet's Hijra; the shrines of Al-Zubeir bin Al-Awam, Talha bin Ubaidillah, Al-Hassan Al-Basri, Ibn Serene, and Ibn Al-Jowzi.

Where to go in Basrah

A lovely spot not to be missed is Sindbad's Island, in the middle of Shatt-Al-Arab (where the river is extremely broad), just opposite Shatt-Al-Arab Hotel. It is connected with the bank by a bridge. The

Island has its own extensive gardens, fountains, casino, refreshment kiosks and chalets, together with an attractive boat restaurant floating nearby.

In Dinar Street, between Ashar and Margil, is the Local Administration Tourist Complex, which covers a total area of 32,800 sq. metres.

It includes a swimming pool, a theatre, a club, a cabaret, a restaurant, a casino, and several residential rooms with up-to-date furnishings, all in the middle of rambling gardens.

The city has several large up-to-date hotels. E. g.:

Arabian Gulf Hotel:

A 6-story, 250-room hotel with 10 suites. It has two swimming pools, several restaurants, a night club, games rooms, and other service and entertainment facilities. Run by the National Tourist Investments Company.

Novotel-Basrah Hotel:

A first class hotel, with 152 double rooms and 8 suites. Reception, lounge, conference hall, restaurant, swimming pool, etc.

SHERATON HOTEL — BASRAH

A 5-star hotel, 6 stories, 207 rooms, 10 suites. All modern facilities, including a night club and a swimming pool.

Basrah is interspersed with several public gardens, notable among which is Andalusia Park (in Margil) which also includes a Luna Park. And, of course, the city has a number of cinemas and night-clubs.

River trips on Shatt-Al-Arab are easy to arrange by simply hiring a motor-boat from the Corniche in Ashar. Here the visitor will find endless "casinos" all along the river where one can have a perfect view of the ships and liners sailing in and out, of the tall palm trees that line the horizon, of the buildings of the University of Basrah glowing in the distance.

Twenty kilometres away, near Zubeir town, spread the 'athal' forests where the people and visitors of Basrah go on day-long picnics under the trees. These song-filled 'athal' outings are an established Basrah tradition.

A TOURIST RESTAURANT — BASRAH

Qurna

Qurna, as legends have it, is the place where the Garden of Eden was. There is an old tree there still called Adam's Tree. 74 kilometres to the north of Basrah, it rises at the confluence of Tigris and Euphrates into one very wide river, Shatt-Al-Arab, amidst extensive fields and palm groves.

The State Organisation for Tourism has put up here a modern Rest House, whose verandas give on to the great expanse of the two rivers.

ADAM'S TREE — QURNA

Abul Khasib

It has also put up a casino at Abul Khasib, the birthplace of the great Iraqi poet, the late Badr Shakir Al-Sayyab, a district which has the highest density of palm trees in the world: a magnificent unforgettable sight. It lies 26 kms. to the south of Basrah, along Shatt-Al-Arab.

Safwan

At Safwan, on the Iraq-Kuwait border, the visitor will find a Rest House and a Tourist Information Centre.

A Tour
in the North

HATRA

SALAHUDDIN GOVERNORATE

As you travel north from Baghdad, on the way to Mosul, you will come across Salahuddin governorate.

There are several important cities and places in this area.

The governorate was called after the great Muslim leader Salahuddin Al-Ayyubi (or Saladin, as he is known in the West), who liberated many parts of the Arab world in his time. He was born in Tikrit in A. D. 1137, and later became King: he reigned over Egypt, Syria and Palestine. He was victorious in the many wars he waged against invaders and intruders in the Arab homeland. His most renowned battle was Hittin, which he won against the Crusaders in Arab Palestine in A. D. 1187.

The centre of the governorate is Tikrit, a city that goes back to ancient times. The Assyrian King Tukulti Ninnurta (ninth century B. C.) and the great Babylonian monarch Nebuchadnezzar (604—562 B. C.) both mentioned the city in their cuneiform inscriptions. In Roman times, it was called Monia Tikrides. In more recent Islamic times it is mentioned in several historical and geographical records. It is nowadays going through a phase of splendid development in construction, industry and agriculture, which includes the city's environs as well.

The other major historical city in this governorate is Samarra.

Samarra

About 74 years after the foundation of Baghdad, the Abbasid Caliph Al-Mu'tasim moved his capital north, to the newly built city of Samarra, in A. D. 836. Its heyday however was under Caliph Al-

Mutawakkil, (A. D. 847—861). In 892 Caliph Al-Mu'tadhid shifted his capital back to Baghdad.

Despite the short sojourn of the Abbasid Caliphate in Samarra, the city's artistic, literary and scientific splendours have remained a legend in Arab history.

The remains of ancient Samarra are visible along the eastern bank of the Tigris, stretching south of the modern city for nearly 35 kms: the Great Mosque, the Spiral Minaret, Balkwara Palace, Ma'shouq Palace, etc. To the north of the Spiral Minaret are the Caliph's Residence, Tell al-Ullaiq, Abu Duluf Mosque, Mutawak-kiliya, Rassasi River — and so on until one arrives at the city of Dour.

Major spots to see: The Great Mosque, the Caliph's Residence, the Askari Shrine, Abu Duluf Mosque, and Ma'shouq Palace.

The Great Mosque:

A dominating, magnificent structure which was once the largest mosque in the Islamic world. It was built by Al-Mutawakkil in A. D.

THE SPIRAL MINARET OF THE GREAT MOSQUE

852 from bricks and clay. It has a rectangular plan measuring 240 × 160 metres, with walls 10 metres high, 2.65 m. thick, supported by 44 towers. The courtyard was surrounded on all sides by an arcade, the greatest part of which was the one facing Mecca.

The Mosque's minaret is the Malwiya ("the Spiral") which rises, 27 metres away from the northern side of the Mosque, to a height of 52 metres. Some historians believe that it pre-dates the Mosque and that it was built by Al-Mu'tasim.

The Caliph's Residence:

Built by Al-Mu'tasim to overlook the Tigris with a front 700 metres long. What remains of it today is a group of three *ewans* giving onto the river, the central one measuring 17.5 × 8 metres, with a height of 12 metres. These *ewans* were called "The Commoners Gate": the Caliph would sit there to hear the people's complaints and suggestions, as Arab caliphs always took personal interest in their citizens' affairs.

Abu Duluf Mosque:

Samarra was penetrated by a very long axial street called Al-Adham ("the Greatest"), at the end of which, 22 kms away from the

ABU DULUF MOSQUE

modern city, are the remnants of a large mosque still mostly extant. It was built by Al-Mutawakkil to look like a smaller version of the Great Mosque, including the "mulwiya" minaret. The pointed arches on the mosque's supports form the only difference in the look of the two mosques. Measuring 215.5×138 m., it has a beautiful courtyard. The minaret is 19 m. high.

Ma'shouq Palace:

About 10 kms. to the north-west of Samarra you can see a brick-built palace called Kasr al-Ma'shouq ("the Beloved's Palace") — some may still call it Kasr Al'Asheq ("the Lover's Palace").

It lies on a high platform, with arches supporting the roof. A spiral path leads to the palace chambers, which are ornamented with clay arabesques. On the exterior are arches and pillars stuck to the walls.

It was built by Al-Mu'tadhid just before he left the city for Baghdad.

The Askari Shrine:

Where the two imams Ali Al-Hadi and his son Hassan Al-Askari are entombed under a golden dome 68 metres in circumference, with two golden minarets 36 metres high.

THE ASKARI SHRINE

NINEVEH GOVERNORATE

The largest governorate in the North. The Assyrians were the first great rulers to build their cities and strongholds in this part of Iraq, which they turned into a base for a vast empire. In Umayyad and Abbasid times this region maintained its importance. The major city of the governorate is Mosul.

VIEW OF MOSUL CITY

Mosul

The north's largest city and its major centre for trade, industry and communications. It has the second largest university in Iraq.

400 kms. from Baghdad, it is linked with the capital by a first-class road, by a railway with a daily trip (from Mosul and Baghdad at 8.30 p.m.), and by regular flights. Automobile and rail routes go through Mosul which connect Iraq with Syria, Turkey and Europe, Mosul is also the starting-point of most of the roads that lead to Iraq's Northern resorts.

Mosul is called "the city of two springs", because autumn and spring are very much alike in it. It is also named Al-Hadba, Al-Faiha, and Al-Khadhra.

The city has been continuously inhabited since Assyrian times. Long before Islam, a number of Arab tribes had settled in it, and in later times it played a leading role in the Arab wars of conquest and became a city of great importance. It is rich in old historical places: castles, mosques, churches, monasteries, schools, most of which abound in architectural features and decorative works of significance.

Mosul today is a large prosperous city spread out on both sides of the Tigris, with all the amenities of modern living and many parks, theatres, hotels, etc.

Since 1969, a Spring Festival has been held every year in Mosul. Flower processions and folk dancing by thousands of people from every walk of life bring much gaiety to the place.

HISTORICAL PLACES IN MOSUL

The Umayyad Mosque:

The first ever in the city, it was built by Utba bin Farqad Al-Salami after he conquered Mosul in the reign of Omar bin Al-Khattab. The only part still extant is the minaret.

The Mujahidi Mosque:

It dates back to the 12th century A. D. and is distinguished for its beautiful dome and elaborately-wrought 'mihrab'.

The Great (Nurid) Mosque:

Built by Nuriddin Zangi in A.D. 1172, it is famed for its remarkably bent minaret, 52 metres high, done in elaborate brickwork and called Al-Hadba ("the Humped").

THE GREAT (NURID) MOSQUE

The Mosque of the Prophet Jonah:

An old mosque popularly believed to be the burial place of Jonah, as it is built on one of the mounds that rise over the ruins of Nineveh.

The Mosque of the Prophet Jerjis:

Believed to be the burial place of Prophet Jerjis, it is difficult to date exactly. The last time it was "renovated" was in A.D. 1393.

Mashad Yahya Abul Kassem:

On the right bank of Tigris, known for its conical dome, decorative brick-work and calligraphy engraved in Mosul blue marble. 13th century.

Qara Serai (The Black Palace):

The remnants of the 13th century palace of Sultan Badruddin Lu'lu'.

QARA SERAI (THE BLACK PALACE)

Bash Tapia Castle:

Part of Mosul's old walls which have disappeared, with the exception of these imposing ruins rising high over Tigris.

CHURCHES AND MONASTERIES

Mosul is noted for its numerous old churches and monasteries, some of which originally date back to the early centuries of Christianity. Examples:

The Church of Simon Peter:

The oldest Chaldean church in Mosul believed to have been built in the 13th century.

Church of Al-Tahira ("The Immaculate"):

Near Bash Tapia, probably the remnants of the church of the Upper Monastery. Reconstructed last in 1743.

Church of St. Thomas:

One of the oldest historical churches, its present structure suggests a 13th century style.

The Roman Catholic Church:

Built by the Dominican Fathers in Nineveh Street in 1893.

St. George's Monastery:

To the north of Mosul. Most probably built late in the 17th century. Pilgrims from different parts of the North visit it annually in the spring, when many people also go out to its environs on holiday.

St. Elijah's Monastery:

To the south of Mosul. Some distance away from the city there are other monasteries, notably:

The Monastery of St. Matti:

At the top of Mount Maqloub, it dates back to the 4th century A. D.

St. Behnam's Monastery:

Also called Deir al-Jubb (the "Cistern Monastery"), in the Nineveh Plain near Nimrud. 12th or 13th century.

THE MOSUL MUSEUM

The Museum is now in a new building, constructed after the 17th July Revolution, near Liberty Bridge.

It has on display a large collection of finds that represent the successive civilizations of Iraq, from the Paleolithic Age up to later Arab Islamic times, with emphasis on archaeological finds discovered in Nineveh Governorate.

THE MOSUL MUSEUM

Forest Tourist Casino:

A first-class spot in the northern corner of the Hadba model forest, on the left bank of the Tigris. Up to date equipment; food and drinks; eastern and western music. The Casino also provides food to the tourist chalets nearby.

FOREST TOURIST CASINO

Waterfalls Tourist Chalets:

They stand about 15 kms. away from the centre of Mosul to the north-east, in beautiful country where the river Khosar comes down in waterfalls. The chalets are in two groups of ten houses each, separated by the water-falls lake. Each is made up of a sitting room, a bedroom, a bathroom and a kitchen, all well-furnished.

Forest Chalets:

There are 35 of them in the middle of Hadba forest. 20 of them are designed for four persons each, the other 15 for 2 persons each. They are all equipped with kitchens and bathrooms and very well-furnished, and S.O.F.T. has seen to it, that they all have heating, cooling, refrigerators, telephones, and TV sets.

THE FORESTS IN MOSUL

AL-GHABBAT RESTAURANT

150

NINEVEH WALL

Nineveh

The city of Nineveh had a glorious history which made the Governorate assume its name. It was the third Assyrian capital after Assur and Nimrud, and its position in the centre of the original Assyrian lands between the rivers Tigris and Zab gave it an added administrative and religious importance. But it had been a cultural settlement since long before, right through Sumerian and Babylonian periods. In fact the name of Nineveh is of Sumerian origin.

Nineveh was ruled by a number of great Assyrian Kings, such as Sargon II (721—705 B.C.), before he moved to Dur Sharrukin (Khorsabad), succeeded by his son Sennacherib (705—681 B.C.) who abandoned his father's new capital and went back to Nineveh, and Esarhaddon (681—669) and Assur-bani-pal (619—626), all of whom enlarged and built up the city and made it the centre of the civilized world of their time. Sennacherib brought water to it in an 80 km. long canal from river Gomel, built a dam for water regulation the remains of which are still visible somewhere near the eastern wall, and filled the city and its environs with gardens and orchards to which he brought some rare trees.

On rising ground you can see the remains of the ancient walls, partly reconstructed, 12 kms. in circumference. There were 15 gates each called after an Assyrian god. The two most prominent mounds of ruins are Koyunjuk and Nabi Younis. On the latter hill rises now the Mosque of Nebi Younis (Jonah). King Esarhaddon had once built a palace on this very hill.

On Koyunjuk hill are the remains of the most important palaces of the period: Sennacherib's palace, with 71 chambers and halls and 27 entrances, embellished with winged bulls and lions. The walls had long series of bas-reliefs most of which were taken to the British Museum, as they were dug up by quite unscientifically by European excavators in the middle of the last century, when Iraq was still under Ottoman domination. Assurbanipal left us some even more magnificent bas-reliefs and a library with thousands of clay tablets which he had collected from various cities and which preserved for us much of the lore and knowledge of ancient Mesopotamia.

The General Establishment of Antiquities and Heritage has worked hard on certain parts of the site and reconstructed Maska and Shamash Gates, and some of the wall, and conserved Sennacherib's Palace. Nergal Gate, after reconstruction, is now used as a small museum where models of leading Assyrian towns are on display.

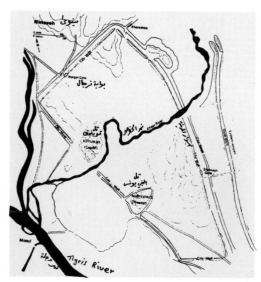

THE CITY PLAN AND FORTIFICATIONS OF NINEVEH IN LATE ASSYRIAN TIMES. EXCAVATIONS IN THE SECOND HALF OF THE 19TH CENTURY TOOK PLACE PRINCIPALLY ON THE MAIN CITADEL MOUND, KÜYÜNJIK.

To help visitors enjoy sightseeing at Nineveh S.O.F.T. has built this casino on one of the mounds near Adad Gate, and given it an Assyrian design. It provides food and drinks, together with a lovely view of the city of Mosul.

NINEVEH CASINO

Nimrud

The second capital of Assyria had been a well-settled place for a thousand years before it was built as a centre of his kingdom by Shalmaneser I (1273—1244 B.C.). A famous king of Nimrud was Assur-nasir-pal II (883—859 B.C.), and so was his son Shalmaneser III (858—824) who constructed its ziggurat together with a temple next to it.

Lying as it does on the east bank of the Tigris, 37 kms. to the south-east of Mosul, the city has a four-side wall measuring in all 8 kms., and several buildings, in the south-western and south-eastern corners, raised on mud-brick platforms as much as forty feet high above river-level. Some of the buildings are: the temple of Ninurta,

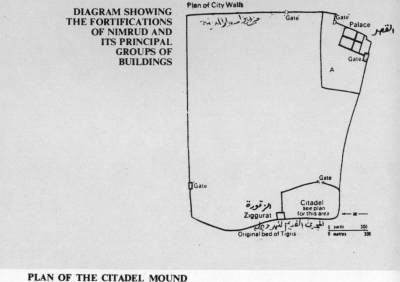

DIAGRAM SHOWING THE FORTIFICATIONS OF NIMRUD AND ITS PRINCIPAL GROUPS OF BUILDINGS

Plan of City Walls

'Gate' 'Gate'

Palace القصر

Gate

A

Gate

Gate

Gate

Citadel
see plan
for this area

Ziggurat الزقورة

Original bed of Tigris

0 yards 300
0 metres 300

PLAN OF THE CITADEL MOUND AT NIMRUD AFTER THE CONCLUSION OF MALLOWAN'S WORK THERE IN 1963

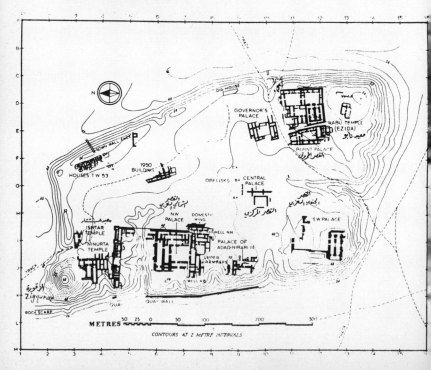

DIG HOUSE

GOVERNOR'S PALACE

NABU TEMPLE (EZIDA)

TOWN WALL EAST

BURNT PALACE

HOUSES TW 53

1950 BUILDING

OBELISKS

CENTRAL PALACE

ISHTAR TEMPLE

NW PALACE

DOMESTIC WING

SW PALACE

NINURTA TEMPLE

WELL NN

PALACE OF ADAD-NIRARI III

UPPER CHAMBERS

WELL AB

QUA

Ziggurat

ROCK SCARP

QUAY WALL

METRES 50 25 0 50 100 200 300

CONTOURS AT 2 METRE INTERVALS

the north-western and the south-western palaces, Sargon's Palace, and others — notably the ziggurat which looks rather like a conical hill, the remains of it rising to a height of 17 metres. It lies in the north-western corner of the city. It originally had a square base, with most probably a spiral ramp like that of Samarra's mulwiya minaret, leading to its upper levels.

IVORY HEAD OF WOMAN FROM NIMRUD (720 B.C.)

Assurnasirpal II's Palace, known as the north-western palace, has an area of 200 × 130 metres, and consists of administration, royal reception, and residential parts. The visitor at present enters the palace through a couple of doorways, between human-headed bulls

NIMRUD, THE FAMOUS CAPITAL OF THE ASSYRIAN EMPIRE

or lions with the wings of a hawk. These huge sculptures were meant
to be the guardians of the city. Some beautiful bas-relief slabs are still
on the site, though most of them were taken away by foreign
excavators. Most striking is the throne room, measuring 45.5 × 10.5

RELIEF FROM NIMRUD

metres. It was here that a large number of exquisite ivory carvings were found, such as the so-called "Mona Lisa of Nirmud" and the piece showing a lioness mauling an Ethiopian, which is gilded and set with lapis-lazuli and agate.

The south-western palace belonged to Esarhaddon. One of the buildings is Esida, the temple of Nabu, god of visdom and the arts and sciences, son of the Babylonian god Marduk. It was the work of Queen Samuramat (Semiramis), mother of Adad-Nirari III (810—782 B.C.).

Dur Sharrukin (Khorsabad)

The fourth capital of Assyria, built by Sargon II (721—705 B.C.) on a square plan with a mud-brick wall with 7 gates. The inside walls of the king's palace were covered with magnificient marble (and some bronze) bas-reliefs, which were taken by the archaeologists to the Louvre in the last century. The massive winged bulls which guarded the doorways were scattered over a number of museums in the world. Two of them are in the Iraq Museum in Baghdad. The palace is in need of much excavation and reconstruction which, it is hoped, are in the offing. The General Establishment of Antiquities, however, has reconstructed the nearby Temple of the Sibitti — "the seven gods" (usually represented by seven small spheres on cylinder seals).

Ironically, this city was not lived in for long: Sargon was killed only one year after he had moved into it, and his son Sennacherib went back to Nineveh and carried away with him many of its sculptures to decorate his palace there.

Assur

The first capital of a people who named their city after their major god, and who in time built a vast empire which included Iraq, Syria, Anatolia, Iran, Egypt and parts of Arabia.

Assur (today called Qalat Shergat) is 11 kms. to the south of Mosul, near Himrin mountains believed by the Assyrians to be the abode of god Assur. It lies on a stony hill overlooking the Tigris on the east. To the north of it is the river's old course. It was fortified by an inner wall and an outside wall, with several gateways.

It had been a human settlement long before it became a capital, and it was known to have come under the dominion of Akkad, of the Third Dynasty of Ur, and of the Babylonians in the 31st year of Hammurabi's reign.

Assur continued to be the Assyrian capital until Ashurnasirpal (883—859 B.C.) removed the seat of power to Nimrud (Kalakh), where his son Shalmaneser III reigned after him. But Assur maintained its religious distinction. Its most striking sight today is the ziggurat, devoted to the god Assur, as well as the ground temple nearby devoted to the same god and called Temple of the Universe. There are also temples devoted to the gods of the sun and the moon, and one with two towers sacred to Anu, god of the sky, and Adad, god of storms.

The city overflowed its walls, and many buildings were erected beyond them, notably the Akitu temple where the New Year Festivals were celebrated. It was built by Sennacherib on the river bank (now the old course of the Tigris) and had it surrounded by extensive gardens.

You can also see a recently reconstructed building: the Arab Palace with the four *ewans* which were once decorated with plaster arabesques. It dates back to the Arab reign in Hatra some two-thousand years ago. In the course of their excavations, Iraqi archaeologists discovered the Arabic name of the architect, who had designed the palace, on one of its supports — which justifies calling it the Arab Palace. On instructions from the Political Leadership a project was initiated in 1978 to revive the city. A number of spots have been selected by the project committee for reconstruction work, and a building was chosen to be a museum for local finds.

THE ASSYRIAN CITY OF ASSUR AS RECONSTRUCTED BY SPECIALISTS

Hatra

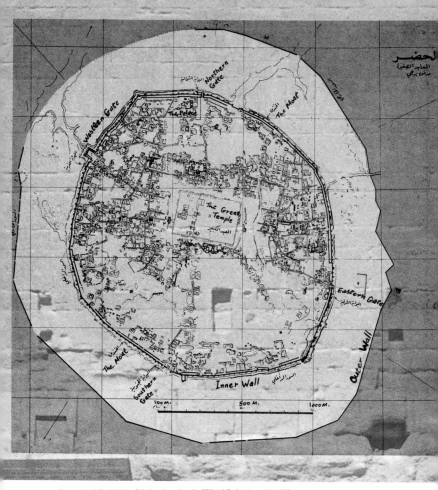

PLAN OF THE GREAT ARAB KINGDOM — HATRA

The ancient Arab city of Hatra, near Wadi Tharthar, is 27 kms. to the west of the Baghdad-Mosul highway, at a point 80 kms. south of Mosul. In architecture, sculpture, metal work, the arts of war, Hatra was no less advanced than Rome. It was another link in the chain of great Arab cities: Palmyra in Syria, Petra in Jordan and Baalbeck in Lebanon, and others.

Although we possess few texts that may tell us about the obscure beginnings of the city, it seems it began actually to grow sometime in the third century B. C. Before the foundation of kingship around A. D. 156, Hatra was governed by Arab rulers who combined religious and secular authority. Prominent among them was Nasr, father of the first two kings of Hatra: Lajash and Sanatruq. The latter was succeeded by his son Abd Samia (A. D. 190—200), who in turn was succeeded by Sanatruq II (A. D. 200—241), the last Arab king of the city.

THE NORTH GATE OF THE GREAT TEMPLE

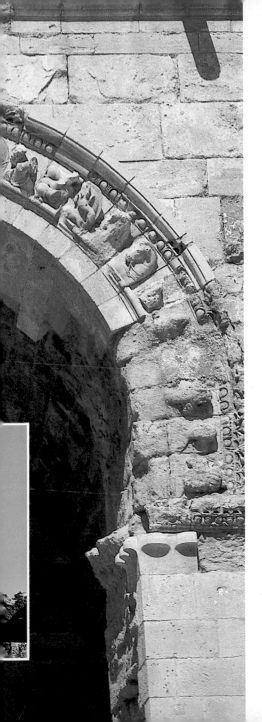

THE ARAB
SCULPTORS OF
HATRA DECORATED
THEIR BUILDINGS

ALABASTER STATUE
OF A GOD FROM
HATRA (160 A.D.)

STATUE OF ABBU
EXHIBITED IN THE
GREAT TEMPLE

Plan and Major Buildings

When the city comes into view you will see an earthen barrier that goes round it with a diametre of about 3 kms., and about 500 metres away from it you will see a great stone wall with tower bastions and four gateways (at the four points of the compass), noted for their oblique entrances, like the gateways of Mansour's Round City of Baghdad.

There is a modern entrance to the city today which leads to the eastern cemetery which has stone structures with vaulted halls — indicating Arab skill in this kind of architecture. A rectangular building follows: it is the huge Great Temple (437.5 × 322.5 metres). When you enter through one of its eastern doorways, you will come to a spacious courtyard which occupied three-quarters of the temple's area. This open space is separated from the gods' quarters by a wall with two triple doors. Opposite the wall is a sanctuary — a room on a platform with a line of columns on either side. On the right is another sanctuary, with three *ewans,* the central one being much bigger than the other two, built by Sanatruq I. It has a frieze with sculptures which seem to tell a religious story enacted by gods and musicians — the most beautiful work of art so far discovered.

When you enter through the southern doors, you come to a group of *ewans* which give an idea of the effort and skill the Arab architects showed in building their city.

Before we discuss those *ewans* facing east, we draw your attention to the temple of the goddess Shahiro ("the morning star") on your right, whose façade is without ornament, in front of which is another temple with three ewans called the Flag Sanctuary. Opposite you will find eight *ewans,* six of which are in two groups of 3 each, one south, and the other north, the middle one in both cases being the largest. Over and behind the smaller *ewans* are the service rooms of the priests of the temple.

Upon entering the large *ewan* of the southern group you will come to an area measuring 30 × 15 metres, paved with veined marble, with walls decorated with geometrical designs and eagles — eagles being the main element in the Hatra religion. Over a decorative frieze on the left is some Arabic writing that dates back to the second half of the Abbasid era. It is the work of a family which ruled in Mosul at the time. In the wall that faces you there is a doorway which leads to the interior of the square-shaped Temple of the Sun God.

The large *ewan* of the northern group is in general a kind of mirror-image of the southern large *ewan*. Moving south, you will come to a temple with also three *ewans:* there is a large pit in front of it believed by some scholars to have been an artificial pond.

Going round the city you will see a large edifice in front of the recently discovered gateway and the eastern gateway which is just off the street. There are about a dozen other smaller temples scattered throughout the city, all bearing a variety of statues and inscriptions.

And now, who were the major gods worshipped by the Arabs here? The Sun god was one, whose temple you have just seen. They also worshipped the eagle and Venus (the morning star) who was called variously Allatu, Atra'ta, and Marthin ("our lady"). Nergoul (the Sumero-Babylonian Nergal), symbolized by the planet Mars, was another of their gods.

The inscriptions in Hatra are in the same alphabet used by Arabs in Palmyra and other Arab cities: it is the Aramaic which spread in most regions of the ancient East. Some inscriptions read as follows: "Kings and princes of Hatra are the victorious kings of the Arabs."

Hatra Rest-House:

Near the remains of the ancient Arab city. It has 20 double rooms, a lounge, two dining halls, and all other ancillaries of comfort. Meals, drinks and refreshments are served to passing visitors.

SHAHIRO SHRINE IN THE GREAT TEMPLE OF HATRA

THE ARAB
ARCHITECTS LEFT
THEIR NAMES
INSCRIBED ON
STONES IN
HATRA

168

زبيده ويه
ولدابرخى ا
ابن بهشتى

ANSHKI SUMMER RESORT

DUHOK GOVERNORATE

At a distance of 73 kms. from Mosul lies Duhok, the centre of the Governorate, at an opening in the mountain also called Duhok.

It is known nation-wide for its vast vineyards and its excellent grapes, figs and pomegranates. Before getting to it the visitor will see an old tell with the ruins of a castle, an indication of an ancient settlement which, most probably, dates back to Assyrian times.

The area is rich in scenic beauty, where nature is lavish with water and vegetation. There are several sites and summer resorts in it, notably the following:

1. Amadiya Antique Castle:

Perched on top of a mountain 1400 metres above sea-level, this impregnable castle played a prominent role in the ancient history of Iraq. It is elliptical in shape, founded on a large rock which is in one piece, surrounded by mountain tops. It has two gates, Zebar Gate — leading to Zebar region and Mosul Gate — leading to Mosul. On the latter gate images are carved portraying warriors with spears, swords and shields; under their feet is a great snake which unwinds itself all the way up to the gate's arch. The castle was called after Imaduddin Zangi, who built it in 537 Hijra. It is about 90 kilometres away from the governorate centre, and the road to it is asphalted and in good condition.

2. The Abbasid Bridge:

This durable well-shaped stone bridge across the Khabour river is considered to be one of the most interesting remains in Iraq.

It is still in a natural state and in constant use — a site popular with tourists. It is 55 kms. away from the governorate centre and has a good asphalted road leading to it.

THE ABBASID BRIDGE

DUHOK GOVERNORATE'S SUMMER RESORTS

1. Zawita:

17 kms. away from Duhok, 90 kms. from Mosul, 885 metres above sea-level, with a maximum temperature of 38°C. Zawita is distinguished for its pine-forests: its extensive shady spots make it particularly attractive in the summer. Its afforestation probably goes back to Assyrian times. Its name is Aramaic, meaning 'Corner'. Somewhere nearby is a wide cleft in the mountain called Gully Zawita. There is a well-furnished rest-house in Zawita.

2. Suara Tuga:

22 kms. from Zawita, 112 kms. from Mosul, 1,507 metres above sea-level, with a maximum temperature of 33°C., it is one of the best-situated summer resorts in the North. It overlooks a deep valley, with higher mountains on either side which seem to give the place a perfect climate, as good as that of any summer resort in the world, with poplars, cypress trees and a variety of summer fruit-trees. There is a large up-to-date hotel, together with a modern casino, in the middle of gardens which give on to two plains, Bamarny and Suara Tuga, between which rises the Suara Tuga chain of mountains. There are also a number of tourist cabins of different sizes, all well-furnished.

3. Ashawa:

Just about 5 kilometres before you get to Sarsang you will come across Ashawa, a lovely summer resort famed for its waterfall. There is a restaurant, together with some local shops.

ASHAWA RESORT

4. Sarsang:

Upon leaving Suara Tuga the road descends east until, a few kilometres away, it hits Bamarny, then Sikreen, famed for its water and vineyards. Some distance away is Sarsang (126 kms. from Mosul), one of the most appealing summer resorts in Iraq. It rises 1,046 metres above sea-level, with a maximum temperature of 34°C.

A lovely climate, cold water cascading from mountain springs, forests of cypress trees and poplars, a diversity of fruit-trees in endless orchards, await the visitor to Sarsang, where there are several government-run touristic establishments:

a) Sarsang Hotel: built on a steep mountain slope overlooking many gardens and orchards. Excellent menus and drinks. Big swimming pool and tennis courts.

b) Tourist Hotel, opposite Grand Hotel: a beautiful spot, with wide verandas giving on to the orchards and forests around. With a swimming pool. Run by the State Organisation for Tourism.

c) Tourist houses.

d) 5 Chalets with 300 beds, a supermarket and a laundry.

e) A Night Club.

f) 50 Popular Chalets.
g) Municipality Hotel.

Throughout the area are lodging rooms, restaurants, super-markets and playgrounds for children together with an open-air cinema and the Revolution Roving Theatre, let alone popular cafés and consumer shops, a post office and a branch of Rafidain Bank.

5. Anshki:

On your way to Amadiya, 15 kms. from Sarsang, you will find Anshki in a lovely spot overlooking the plains of Sarsang. Anshki is

SARSANG RESORT　　　　　**SARSANG HOTEL**

noted for its cool climate and tumbling waterfalls, which run through the casinos and eating places of the village.

A tourist complex in this summer resort includes the following:

a) furnished apartments with a capacity of 288 beds;
b) the Tourist Cave Restaurant which can serve 130 persons;
c) a supermarket;
d) a night club.

6. Araden:

Close to Anshki. This resort has a healthy climate, plentiful

THE CAVE RESTAURANT   **SULAF HOTEL**

waters, and beautiful nature, all at a height of 1400 metres above sea-level, 144 kms. away from Mosul.

7. Sulaf:

In a beautiful valley in the mountains, 5 kms. before Amadiya, is Sulaf, 1,150 metres high above sea-level, with gorgeous waterfalls, one of which cascades from a height of 25 metres. Sulaf is noted for its plentiful fruit trees and the large number of its natural caves — notably Al-Safa Cave, heavily shaded by walnut trees.

There are a number of privately-owned restaurants and hotels besides the 26-rooms Sulaf Hotel put up by S.O.F.T., which has all the conveniences of comfort, including a swimming pool, and commands a view of Amadiya and Sarsang mountains. S.O.F.T. has also recently built a casino, a restaurant and tourist apartments enough for a 130 persons. A good 166 kms. road, well asphalted, connects Sulaf with Mosul.

8. Amadiya:

37 kms. away from Sarsang, at a height of 1985 metres above sea-level, is Amadiya: on top of the mountains which rise high above the whole district — endless green valleys and fertile plains.

All the above, and more: In all the administrative centres of Duhok governorate you will find public gardens, children's playgrounds, swimming pools, modern shops, public libraries, and cinemas.

175

KURDISH DANCE

SULAIMANIYA GOVERNORATE

Sulaimaniya Governorate is famed for its woods and forests and especially its walnut trees which are particularly plentiful in Bibyara and Twaila. These two villages are also famed, apart from natural beauty, for their vineyards.

The oldest cultural settlements in this area go back to paleolithic times. When written history begins we find that the Assyrians called this governorate and Shahrazour Plain by the name of "Samwa." In Derbandkawa, Kara Dagh mountains, the Akkadian king Naram Sin (2291—2255) immortalized his victory over the enemy in a famous stela of great artistry.

Shahrazour Plain, one of the most fertile in the north, is about

2000 square kms. in area, bounded on the north by Hoṃan mountains, which the Arabs once called Jibal Sha'ran, and on the south by Diyala river. The Arabs lived in these parts long before Islam, and one of the tribes here was Banu Sheiban. The Hatra Arabs fought fierce battles with the Persians and defeated them in the Battle of Shahrazour in the first half of the 3rd century A. D.

The governorate's centre is Sulamaniya, which was built by an Ottoman **wali** called Sulaiman Pasha the Great, in 1780. It is 900 metres high above sea-level, in the middle of a mountain chain. It has two approaches: one from Kirkuk, by a 365 km. road, and the other from Baquba, Jelawa, Derbendikhan, by a 333 km. road. Both roads are well built.

Sulaimaniya Hotel:

Built by S.O.F.T. in the heart of the city, this first-class hotel was inaugurated in the July 1979 festivities. It is a large 9 story air-conditioned building with all the up-to-date services and comforts, together with 60 single and double rooms and 6 suites. It has a 500 seat conference hall, suitable for public performances as well, apart from a restaurant and a casino situated on the top floor.

SULAIMANIYA HOTEL

SARCHINAR RESORT

MAJOR RESORTS IN SULAIMANIYA GOVERNORATE

1. Sarchinar:

5 kms. from Sulaimaniya, this summer resort lies amidst tall trees and flowing waters. There are several tourist houses, hotels and casinos.

2. Dokan Lake:

71 kms. from Sulaimaniya, 141 kms. from Kirkuk. A large beautiful blue lake, with a rest-house and a number of restaurants and cafés.

3. Derbendikhan Lake:

65 kms. from Sulaimaniya, 268 kms. from Baghdad. Excellent for boating, with tourist facilites.

4. Ahmad Awa:

A delightful mountain resort accessible by a paved road 75 kms. long off Sulaimaniya.

▲
DOKAN RESORT

▲
SUNSET IN DOKAN

▶
◀ **DOKAN LAKE**

ARBIL FORTRESS

ARBIL GOVERNORATE

This governorate is of great historical importance, and because of its main city's prominence the Revolution Command Council has made it the seat of the Autonomous Region in order to secure for all national groups the right of full self-expression within the frame-work of one unified land, where reigns mutual respect among these brotherly groups.

Early in this guide we said something about this part of the country being the most important place in the world for the study of the culture of Neanderthal man, 35,000—70,000 years ago. Cunei-form inscriptions suggest that Arbil was very well-known towards the end of the 3rd millennium B. C. Syrian inscriptions of the second millennium refer to it as Urbilum or Arbilum. In Assyrian and Babylonian texts it is called Arba Ilu ("the four gods"). It was a centre of the worship of Ishtar, whose temple was called E-kshan-klama ("House of the Lady of the Regions"); there was in it also a temple devoted to the god Assur. A stela of Ashurbanipal (668—627 B.C.) was unearthed in it, together with images of other Assyrian kings. Sennacherib (705—681) built an irrigation canal which carried water down to the city from Bastura Valley, 20 kms. away. The valley will be seen by the visitor as he drives to Salahuddin summer resort. At Bastura where the canal starts there is a well-built stone wall with a cuneiform transcription which reads: "I, Sennacherib king of Assyria have dug three rivers in Khani Mountains above Arbil, home of the venrated Lady Goddess Ishtar, and made their courses straight."

In Islamic times Arbil flourished again. Arab historians mention its fortress which has been reconstructed by the General Establishment of Antiquities and Heritage. It rises upon a great mound which hides several layers of ancient pre-Islamic settlements.

Arbil has an old minaret, called Mudhaffariya after its governor Mudhaffaruddin (died A. D. 1132). Belonging to a large mosque no more extant, its decorative brickwork is rather similar to that of the Nurid Mosques in Mosul and Dakouk.

The city is almost half-way between Mosul and Kirkuk: 86 kms. away from the former, 93 from the latter.

▲
HANDMADE CARPETS IN ARBIL   **VILLAGE IN THE NORTH**

SALAHUDDIN RESORT

ARBIL GOVERNORATE'S MAJOR RESORTS

1. Salahuddin:

Built on Mount Pirmam, overlooking the plain which stretches as far as Arbil on the one hand, and Mount Safin on the other, it is 32 kms. away from Arbil. Height above sea-level: 1090 metres; maximum temperature in the summer: 36°C.

SARA RUSH THEATRE ▶

◀ SALAHUDDIN RESTAURANT

One of the loveliest spots in the country with its cypress and oak trees, it has been the object of special interest on the part of the authorities. Development projects and service amenities in it are being daily expanded and multiplied.

The first thing you see is the Tourist Camp with its information office. The tourist chalets are all beautifully furnished and well-equipped.

After the Camp you will come to the centre of the town where the main offices are, together with a variety of shops which provide visitors with all the requirements of a happy stay.

185

▲
TOURIST HOUSES

Tourist Facilities:

a) The Tourist Village, a group of 39 houses (capacity: 200 beds) with excellent services.

b) Salahuddin Hotel: A first-class hotel, with a large lounge and a large dining room, in the middle of extensive gardens. Well-equipped for holiday-makers.

c) Salahuddin Restaurant: 120 seats.

d) Tourist Sports Hall: Capacity, 70 persons.

Salahuddin, moreover, has shops, booksellers, a filling station, gardens, children's playgrounds, schools, a hospital, a people's clinic, pharmacies, a cinema, a post office, together with several privately-owned hotels, such as Bekhal, Koran, Sherene, Rasoul, Janurouk.

◀ **THE TOURIST VILLAGE**

TOURIST APARTMENTS
▼

2. Sara Rush:

The nearest resort to Salahuddin — only 9 kms. away on a well-built road — where temperature is 5 to 8 degrees lower than in Salahuddin. It has several touristic installations, mainly:

a) Sara Rush hotel — 200 beds
b) Mada' in Tourist Village — 400 beds.
c) Chalets (Ur Houses) — 216 beds.
d) Chalets (Sulaf Houses) — 180 beds.
e) Chalets (Hatra Houses) — 588 beds.
f) Residential apartments — 300 persons.
g) A hall — 320 persons.
h) A restaurant — 150 persons.

Sara Rush has also a supermarket, a folklore shop, children's playgrounds, excursion gardens, etc.

TOURIST BUNGALOWS

▲
SARA RUSH HOTEL

◀ **THE TOURIST VILLAGE**

3. Shaqlawa:

Some 18 kms. away from Salahuddin, this summer resort lies on a slope of Mount Safin at 966 metres above sea-level, with a maximum temperature of 35°C. A place of great scenic beauty with many mountain tops around it, and rich in orchards: walnuts, almonds, pomegranates, grapes, apples, pears, all grow in profusion here, together with endless poplars and cypresses. Here is shade that indeed spreads far and wide.

Some of its tourist facilities:

a) Shaqlawa Hotel — 94 beds.
b) Shaqlawa Tourist Village — like that of Salahuddin — 200 beds.
c) Tourist Camp — 76 beds (two to each tent), with bathrooms and a kitchen.

There are also several privately-owned hotels: Mashkour, Baghdad, Rashid, Jumhouriya, Salim, Othman, Shahrazad, together with popular coffee-shops and restaurants.

Parts of the fruit orchards may be rented by visitors for camping.

HARIR PLAINS

SHAQLAWA RESORT

4. The Plain of Harir Batass:

After you have visited Shaqlawa a good road will take you down to Harir — a village in the Plain of Harir Batass, famed for its exceptional fertility and plentiful waters, for its excellent honey and tobacco, towered over on the right by the Harir mountain range. In between the few farming villages you will see many ancient tells that date back to different ages in the country's history. On the right, there is a large rock sculpture, 50 metres high and 2.5 metres wide, showing a man standing with a conical hat and long wide trousers stretching out his right arm, with a long spear beside him.

The road climbs up to Spillik Mountains (an extension of Harir

SHAQLAWA TOURIST VILLAGE

Mountains), thickly covered with oak-trees. Winding up several times, the road finally drops down to Khleifan village, 21 kms. away from Harir, in a valley where one of the tributaries of river Zab flows, 2 kms. away from the mouth of the famous mountain pass Gully Ali Beg. A road branches out to the left leading up to Shanidar, which acquired world fame when in a cave, the largest of its kind in northern Iraq, skeletons were found belonging to Neanderthal man. The Shanidar cave was a habitation for shifting tribes and shepherds in the early Paleolithic age.

5. Gully Ali Beg and its Waterfall:

This is a place of such striking beauty: one must see it. The Gully is a narrow 10 km. long pass between Mount Kork and Mount Nwathnin, 60 kms. away from Shaqlawa. The mountain view is made even more gorgeous by a fantastic waterfall which tumbles down from a spot 800 metres high above sea-level. Near it is a casino-restaurant. Also, a few trailers for rent by visitors.

GULLY ALI BEG WATERFALL

BEIKHAL WATERFALLS

6. Beikhal Waterfalls:

About 10 kms. beyond Rawanduz, the visitor will come across a great roaring waterfall pouring down from mountain tops in a green cool spot thick with trees all around. Accessible by a road built recently between the Gully and Mount Kork. A small casino for refreshments.

193

7. Jindian:

From Rawanduz it is a short jump to Jindian, another sylvan spot with fresh spring waters. A casino has been built as a nucleus for more developed touristic facilities in future for the area.

8. Derbendi Rayat:

On the way to Haj Omran, about 50 kms. from Gully Ali Beg, it has an up-to-date tourist hotel together with other touristic amenities.

SNOW VIEW IN HAJ OMRAN RESORT

9. Haj Omran:

On the north-east border, to the east of Mount Hassarost, 69 kms. from the Gully's water-fall. This summer resort, 1,780 metres above sea-level, is very cool at night but remarkably temperate by day, with a maximum temperature of 28°C.

In winter, the temperature drops down sharply, to 15°C. below zero, and snow falls. This makes Haj Omran ideal for skiing, which attracts many tourists.

KIRKUK HOTEL

TA'MIM GOVERNORATE

This governorate played a major role in man's early history from early Paleolithic times (100,000 years ago) in Parda Balka, down to the Neolithic age (8,000 years ago).

The earliest farming village in the world, where man learned to plant seeds for the first time, is Jarmo, near Chamchamal in this part of Iraq. Another spot of ancient historical interest is Nuzi Yorgan Tappeh, 25 kms. to the south-east of Kirkuk, the centre of the governorate, where excavators discovered dwellings, a temple, a palace, cuneiform inscriptions of a legal and economic nature, all of which go back to the middle of the second millennium B. C. This period was noted for its particularly fine pottery which has been called after the village. Even more ancient traces here go back to the Sumerians and Akkadians, who called the town Ga-Sur. It was here that the most ancient map in the world was found — it belonged to the Akkadian Era, 4,300 years ago.

In Kirkuk you will see the Castle, one of its oldest extant monuments.

7

General
Information

HOW TO GET TO IRAQ?

LAND ROUTES TO NEIGHBOURING COUNTRIES.

PASSPORT FORMALITIES.

HEALTH REGULATIONS.

CUSTOMS REGULATIONS.

MOTOR VEHICLES.

INSURANCE.

TRAFFIC RULES.

FUEL PRICES.

CURRENCY.

BANKS.

COMMUNICATIONS AND TRANSPORT

BOOKING

GOVERNMENT OFFICE HOURS.

SHOPPING.

OFFICIAL HOLIDAYS.

UNIVERSITIES IN IRAQ.

FOOD AND BEVERAGES.

SERVICE.

HOTEL STAFF DEVELOPMENT

How to get to Iraq?

Geographically, Iraq is a bridge between East and West, accessible from almost all parts of the world by air, land and sea.

With the countries of the Far East Iraq is linked by sea through the Arabian Gulf, by air through regular flights scheduled by Iraqi Airways and other international airlines, and by land via Iran, Afghanistan and so on eastward. Regular international flights connect Baghdad with most European capitals. But one can travel by land from Baghdad northward to Zakho, then Turkey, Bulgaria, and the rest of the European continent. The Orient Express makes two trips a week to and from Baghdad via Syria and Turkey (Istanbul). By sea from Europe, one can go to Beirut, then by land across Syria, or by air, to Baghdad.

LAND ROUTES TO NEIGHBOURING COUNTRIES

1. To Jordan:

A good paved road: Baghdad, Ramadi, Rutba, H.4, Mafraq, Amman (918 kms.)

2. To Syria:

Four major roads:
a) Baghdad, Ramadi, Rutba, Syrian border, Abu Shamat, Damascus. (A good paved road, 835 kms)
b) Baghdad, Ramadi, Rutba, Jordanian border, H.4, Mafraq, Der'a, Damascus. (Paved, 572 kms. to the Iraqi-Jordanian border).
c) Baghdad, Ramadi, Heet juncture, Haditha, Ana, Qaim, Syrian border, Aleppo. (Much of it still under construction, 884 kms.).
d) Baghdad, Mosul, Kasak Rabia, Tell Kochak, Syrian border, Aleppo (Paved, 1,066 kms).

3. To Kuwait:

A good paved road (165 kms. from Basrah): Baghdad, Kut, Amara, Qurna, Basrah, Safwan (on the Kuwaiti border), Kuwait.

4. To Saudi Arabia:

A desert paved road always suitable to motor traffic.

The road more in use internationally, which is paved, is the one connecting Basrah with Safwan, thence across Kuwaiti territory to Saudi Arabia.

5. To Turkey:

A good paved road: Baghdad, Mosul, Zakho, across the Tigris at Fishkabour, where it joins Turkish roads to Diarbakr and Ankara. (From Baghdad to Ankara, 1,786 kms).

6. To Iran:

Two roads, in order of importance:
a) Baghdad, Baquba, Khanaqin, Mundhiriya, Kasr Shirin, Kermanshah, Hamadan, Teheran. (A good asphalted road, 960 kms).
b) Basrah, Shatt-Al-Arab, Qadha, Huwaija, Muhammara (Khurumshar), or Basrah, Abul Khasib, Seeba, thence across Shatt Al-Arab to Abadan.

PASSPORT FORMALITIES

To enter Iraq, a valid passport is required. It must not carry an Israeli visa.

Citizens of Arab countries are not subject to the Residence Law. They may enter Iraq without a visa, reside in Iraq for as long as they wish, and depart without referring to the Residence Department.

For other citizens passport with an entry visa is required, except for Yugoslav subjects who need no entry visa but are subject to Iraq's Residence Law.

HEALTH REGULATIONS

The following health certificates are required from foreigners visiting Iraq:

Cholera

For arrivals from epidemic areas, with the exception of children under 12 months, a vaccination certificate valid 6 days after the first vaccination and for 6 months after the second.

Yellow Fever

For arrivals from epidemic or previously epidemic areas: a vaccination certificate valid 10 days after vaccination for 10 years.

Smallpox

For arrivals from epidemic or previously epidemic areas, with the exception of children under 12 months: a vaccination certificate valid 8 days after first successful vaccination for 3 years.

CUSTOMS REGULATIONS

A tourist may have the following admitted duty-free: 200 cigarettes, 50 cigars, 250 gms. of tobacco, 1 litre of wine or alcoholic beverage, 1 litre of perfume. Also: one camera, one radio, one recorder, with the provision that he shall take them out with him on departure.

MOTOR VEHICLES

Automobiles and motorcycles are admitted against a valid international automobile certificate recognized by the Iraqi Automobile Association in Baghdad, or against a financial security guaranteed by the National Insurance Co.

The period for which automobiles and motorcycles are allowed to stay in Iraq is two months, which may be extended for compelling reasons to a maximum period of one year. Customs duty is imposed at the expiry of this period.

INSURANCE

Any vehicle entering Iraq shall be insured locally against third party injuries. The appropriate insurance policy is issued by the National Insurance Company and is obtainable at the border.

TRAFFIC RULES

Driving in Iraq is on the right-hand side. International traffic signs are used on all Iraqi roads.

FUEL PRICES

Fuel is available at filling stations in every town in Iraq and on major roads, usually at 50 kms. intervals.

There are 2 kinds of petrol: Regular, at 40 fils a litre; Super, at 60 fils a litre. Diesel is available at 20 fils a litre.

CURRENCY

The unit of Iraqi currency is the Dinar, which is divided into 1,000 smaller units called "fils". Currency is either in coins: 1 fils, 5 fils, 10 fils, 25 fils, 50 fils, 100 fils, 250 fils, (or $\frac{1}{4}$ dinar); or in paper notes: $\frac{1}{4}$ dinar, $\frac{1}{2}$ dinar, one dinar, 5 dinars, 10 dinars, 25 dinars.

CURRENCY REGULATIONS FOR VISITORS

Currency	Allowed on entry	Allowed on Departure
Iraqi	ID.25	ID.5
Foreign	No limit (except Israeli currency). If visitor intends to take out amounts brought by him into Iraq a declaration on the proper Exchange Form is required.	
Travellers Cheques	Idem.	

BANKS

Central Bank, Rashid St., Baghdad. Telephone 8871101.

Central Bank, Basrah.

Central Bank, Mosul.

Rafidain Bank, Head Office, Bank St., Baghdad, Telephone 8870244.

Rafidain Bank has 63 branches in Baghdad; 59 branches in Governorates; 7 branches abroad.

Banking Hours

Summer:	Saturday to Wednesday:	8.30 am.—12.30p.m.
	Thursday:	8.30a.m.—11.30a.m.
Winter:	Saturday to Wednesday:	9.00a.m.—1.00p.m.
	Thursday:	9.00a.m.—12. noon.

For Foreign Exchange transactions please go to authorized Rafidain Bank Branches.

Certain Rafidain Bank Branches operate after hours.

These Branches are at:

Baghdad International Airport — International Railway Station — Baghdad Hotel — Khayam Hotel — Diwan Hotel — Alwiya Club — Tourist Centre (Liberation Square) — Qaim (Iraqi-

Syrian border) — Rutba (Iraqi-Syrian-Jordanian border) — Mundhiriya (Iraqi-Iranian border) — Safwan (Iraqi-Kuwaiti border).

COMMUNICATIONS AND TRANSPORT

Taxis are plentiful. Major towns have excellent bus services. A network of well-paved roads connects Baghdad with all parts of the country. Regular flights are scheduled between Baghdad, Basrah and Mosul, for information about which please contact Iraqi Airways Offices and any other travel agencies.

A network of railway lines also connects Baghdad with many towns as well as cities abroad, as follows:

1. Baghdad — Basrah (Margil) — Um Qasr Line, 582 kms., built recently to replace the old Narrow Gauge line. It goes through Babylon (Hilla), Kadisiya (Samawa, thence to Warka). Thi Qar (Nasiriya, thence to Ur), the Marshes with their unique scenic beauty, and Basrah. There are two Baghdad-Basrah and Basrah-Baghdad trains daily, a morning one and an evening one.

2. Baghdad — Baquba — Kirkuk — Arbil Line, 461 kms., including its branches to Jelawla and Khanaqin.

3. Baghdad — Samarra — Tikrit — Shergat, (Ashur) — Hammam al-Alil (mineral baths) — Mosul Line. There are two Baghdad — Mosul and Mosul — Baghdad trains daily, a morning one and an evening one.

4. Baghdad — Mosul — Tell Kochek — Ya'rubiya Line, 528 kms. At the Iraqi border it joins the Syrian and Turkish railways. This Orient Express makes two trips a week from Baghdad to Istanbul and from Istanbul to Baghdad.

Timetable is as follows:

Station	Arrival	Departure	Days
Baghdad	—	20.30	Monday & Friday.
Mosul	6.30	8.35	Tuesday & Saturday.
Ya'rubiya	11.50	12.45	Tuesday & Saturday.
Aleppo	5.15	6.45	Wednesday & Sunday.
Ankara	7.44	8.10	Thursday & Monday.
Istanbul	19.05	—	Thursday & Monday.

Note: The Orient Express train leaves Istanbul every Thursday and Sunday at 10.40 a.m. and arrives in Baghdad at 8.40 the next Sunday and Wednesday respectively.

BOOKING

All train bookings can be made at the Baghdad International Station either directly or by telephone. Call 39962 for booking details.

For any information regarding Iraqi Railways, call 39962.

GOVERNMENT OFFICE HOURS

Iraqi time is 3 hours ahead of Greenwich Meantime.

Summer Office Hours:	8.00 a.m.—2.00 p.m. Weekdays.
	8.00 a.m.—1.00 p.m. Thursdays.
Winter Office Hours:	8.30 a.m.—2.30 p.m. Weekdays.
	8.30 a.m.—1.30 p.m. Thursdays.

As of 1982 summer time begins in Iraq on 1st April by advancing the clock by one hour at midnight, and ends on 30th September by putting the clock back by one hour at midnight.

Office hours during the month of Ramadhan begin one hour later in all government departments and establishments, except for those whose work requirements demand otherwise.

SHOPPING

Most shops are open daily 9.00 a.m.—1.00 p.m. and 4.00—8.00 p.m. They generally close on Fridays.

OFFICIAL HOLIDAYS

The week-end holiday in Iraq is Friday, when Government Offices, semi-official establishments and most public firms are closed. The following are official holidays:

— Id al-Fitr: 3 days.
— Id al-Adha: 4 days.
— Hejira New Year's Day.
— Ashoura Day.

— The Prophet's Birthday.
— New Year's Day.
— Iraqi Army's Day, 6th January.
— 14th Ramadhan Revolution Anniversary, 8th February.
— Spring Day (Nawrooz), 21st March.
— Labour Day, 1st May.
— 14th July, 1958 Revolution Anniversary.
— 17th July, 1968 Revolution Anniversary.

Moreover, all religious communities have the right, ensured by Iraqi Law, to celebrate their major religious feast days as officially recognized holidays.

UNIVERSITIES IN IRAQ

Education in Iraq, in all its stages, is free of charge. Moreover, all text books and other student requirements are given free to students throughout their scholarly career.

Iraqi Universities are made up of a large number of colleges, institutes and educational centres, where arts and science subjects are taught up to the B.A., and Ph.D. levels.

There are also many specialized institutes where undergraduates study subjects related to industry, agriculture, social studies and economics, as part of a plan to meet the country's ever-expanding requirements in all these fields.

As a result of compulsory education in the country, Iraqi Universities have been developing and expanding very rapidly. The major universities are:

1. Baghdad University, in Baghdad.
2. Mustansiriya University, in Baghdad.
3. Technological University, in Baghdad.
4. Al-Bakr University, in Baghdad.
5. Mosul University, in Mosul.
6. Basrah University, in Basrah.
7. Salahuddin University, in Arbil.
8. Kufa University, in Kufa.

FOOD AND BEVERAGES

Iraqi Cuisine is enormously varied.

There are first the popular places which traditionally specialize in certain dishes, such as Kebab grills (including grilled liver and hearts), "guss", tripe, Mosul Kubba, etc.

Then there are the first-class restaurants where, besides Western food, delicious Iraqi dishes are served, e.g., stuffed quzi (grilled whole lamb stuffed with rice, almonds, raisins and spices). If the weather is favourable and you go to one of the innumerable "casinos" along the river-drive called Abu Nuwas Street, you will enjoy mazgouf fish, grilled on an open circular fire of tamarisk wood before you, with thousands of coloured lights shimmering in the Tigris waters.

Tea is the national hot drink, commonly served in small istikans. Coffee comes next in popularity. Soft drinks and juices are of course plentiful.

Liquor is available throughout the country. Apart from the usual internationally known brands, served in licensed hotels, restaurants, bars and "casinos", Iraq has its own popular drink, arrak, which is made from dates or grapes and flavoured with aniseed or mistaki. Iraqi beer is particularly good, and red and white wines are made locally.

SERVICE

In most hotels and restaurants a 10 per cent charge is added to the bill to cover service.

HOTEL STAFF DEVELOPMENT

In order to have an efficient staff service in hotels, S.O.F.T. has established the Baghdad Institute of Tourism and Hotel Services in the capital. Study at this institute is in two stages, basic and advanced, each covering a number of years after primary and intermediate secondary school education.

TELEX

Hotels charge 20% of telex fees in addition to the official tariff for telex communications ensured by their own telexes.

MEDICAL CARE

Medical care is provided to tourists free of charge in the State hospitals and dispensaries.

There are many private clinics and specialized doctors' cabinets which charge for their services.

WATER

The water piped into your hotel room is drinkable. It has been properly treated and purified by the Water Supply Department.

LAUNDRY

Laundry shops are plentiful throughout the country.

WHAT TO WEAR

Iraq's climate varies in accordance with the four seasons.

Winter:

In December, January and February, it tends to be cold. Temperatures may sometimes drop to below zero centigrade. Warm woollen clothes are then necessary. Overcoats, or raincoats may in some days be advisable.

Spring:

In March, April and May the climate is temperate. Light woollen or cotton clothes are worn. A raincoat may sometimes be necessary.

Summer:

In June, July, August, light cotton clothes are generally worn.

Autumn:

In September, October and November, clothes are worn like those in Spring.

ELECTRIC CURRENT

A.C. 220 vt.

HAIRDRESSERS AND BEAUTY SALONS

Usually open from 9.00 a.m. to 8.00 p.m. daily, except on Mondays.

NATIONAL TOURIST BUREAU

The largest travel agency and tour operator in Iraq. It belongs to the socialist sector. It offers full tourist services, like reservations, ticketing and — travel information. It organizes sightseeings and excursions within Iraq and group travel abroad.

The branches of the Bureau spread in major cities of the Country.

THE BRANCHES OF NATIONAL TOURIST BUREAU

	Telephone №
National Tourist Bureau, Sa'doun.	7761990, 779306
National Tourist Bureau, Tahrir Sq.	8870237, 8888192
National Tourist Bureau, Nasr Sq.	8875447
National Tourist Bureau, Mansour.	5514700

	Telephone №
National Tourist Bureau, Kadhimiya.	4416272
National Tourist Bureau, Karbala.	322077
National Tourist Bureau, Nineveh.	2050
National Tourist Bureau, Basrah.	219646
National Tourist Bureau, Hilla.	223684
National Tourist Bureau, Sulaimaniya.	26160
National Tourist Bureau, Kirkuk.	216614

TRAVEL AGENCIES

	Telephone
1. National Tourist Bureau	7760615
2. Orientours Co.	93770
3. Thomas Cook & Son. Ltd.	88921/2
4. Baz Commercial Co.	8889333
5. Levant Express	72751/3
6. Aladdin Travels	811590

	Telephone
7. Saada Travel & Tourism, Abu Qlam	96770
8. Mannar for Transport Tourism	92022
9. International Tours Co.	93891
10. Al-Mansour Travel Co.	93891
11. Baghdad Tours	8885754
12. Ali for Transport, Nidhal St.	

Note: Unless otherwise indicated, the following Agencies have their main offices in Sa'doun Street, Baghdad.

TRAVEL AGENCIES

	Telephone			Telephone
13. Dima Tourism & Transport Co.	8885358		34. Firnass, Abu Nuwas Street.	8889217
14. Bahjat Hassan Travel Co.	8886446		35. Al-Dhahi	8877000
15. United Travel Co.	888687		36. Mohammad Amin, Rukhaita	93695
16. Mohammad Hussein Haddad			37. The Blue Arrow	8878556
Travel & Tourism	8883554		38. Ibn Batouta	8883359
17. Caravan	8881299		39. Eden Travel & Tourism	98668
18. Al-Khayyam	8875181		40. Granada	97645
19. Abul Timman Travel Bureau	8877393		41. Al-Rifa'i	96448
20. Ramadhan & Sons	8889741		42. Basrah International Transport Co.	8871673
21. Gailani Agency for Travel & Tourism	8887181		Basrah International Transport Basrah	212140
22. Dalia	8875880		43. Sindbad for Trade & Tourism	8880913
23. Alloush	8880252		44. Sumer for Tourism & Trade	94296
24. Sahara	8882451		45. Al-Azzawi, Salhiya	31888
25. Ashbelia (Seville)	8871793		46. Haddad Travel & Transport Wathba Sq.	8885653
26. Semiramis	8888114		47. Al-Iktisad Trans-Desert Transport,	
27. Marsoumi	8885474		Salhiya.	33129
28. Tomah for Transport & Tourism, Karbala	322114		48. Al-Andalus International	
29. Akkad, Kadhimiya	4412489		Tours & Transport, Salhiya.	39398
30. Baghdad Cooperative for			49. Al-Ugaily Travel & Transport,	
Travel & Tourism	8870518		Kadhimiya	4419444
	882418		Al-Ugaily Travel & Transport, Salhiya	3296

50. Al-Najaf Travel & Transport, Salhiya ... 8881284
51. Al-Najaf Travel & Transport, Salhiya ... 37696

AUTOMOBILE ROADS FOR TOURISTS

Name of Road	Road №	Distance in Kms.
Baghdad—Samarra—Tikrit—Beiji—Mosul.	1	400
Baghdad—Samarra (Malwiya Restaurant).	1	124
Samarra—Tikrit (Um al-Qura Rest House).	1	51
Tikrit—Beiji (Rest House).	1	43
Beiji—Balalij (to Shergat).	1	56
Balalij Junction—Shergat (Ashur site).	—	26
Balalij Junction—Hatra Junction.	1	42
Hatra Junction—Hatra site (Hotel).	—	27
Hatra Junction—Hammam al-Alil Junction	1	62
Hammam al-Alil Junction—Hammam al-Alil (Mineral Baths).	—	22
Hammam al-Alil Junction—Mosul (Nineveh site).	1	22
Mosul—al-Kasar site — Tell Kuchuk (Syrian border, thence to Aleppo).	1	115
Mosul—Khorsabad (Dur Sharrukin site) & Nuran Waterfalls	—	18
Mosul—Nimrud (Kalakh site)	—	34
Mosul—Aqra	—	91
Mosul—Zakho	2	108
Zakho—Turkish Border	2	11
Mosul—Duhok—Sarsang—Amadiya	—	162
Mosul—Duhok	2	73
Duhok—Zawita (Rest House)	—	23
Zawita—Swara Tuga	—	17
Swara Tuga—Sarsang	—	22
Sarsang—Sulaf	—	22
Sulaf—Amadiya	—	5
Mosul—Eskikalak—Arbil	2	86
Baghdad—Kirkuk—Arbil	2	350
Baghdad—Khalis	2	60
Khalis—Tuz Khormatu	2	120
Tuz Khormatu—Kirkuk	2	75
Kirkuk—Altun Kopri (Popular Crafts)	2	44

AUTOMOBILE ROADS FOR TOURISTS

Name of Road	Road №	Distance in Kms.
Altun Kopri—Arbil	2	51
Arbil—Salahuddin—Shaqlawa	3	50
Arbil—Salahuddin (Summer Resort)	3	32
Salahuddin—Shaqlawa	3	18
Shaqlawa—Harir	3	26
Harir—Gully Ali Beg Waterfall (Restaurant)	3	34
Gully Ali Beg Waterfall—Gallala—Derbendi Rayat—Haj Omran (Summer Resort)	3	71
Haj Omran—Iranian Border (thence to Tebriz)	3	7
Baghdad—Baquba—Khanaqin	5	170
Baghdad—Khan Bani Saad—Baquba	5	66
Baquba—Miqdadiya	5	42
Miqdadiya—Sudour (Rest House Miqdadiya—Saadiya).	5	33
Saadiya—Khanaqin (Rest House)	5	29
Khanaqin—Mundhiriya (Iranian Border, thence to Teheran)	5	9
(Iranian Border, thence to Muhammara)	—	18
Baghdad—Kut—Hai—Nasiriya	6/7	355
Kut—Hai—Nasiriya (Rest House)	7	185
Nasiriya—Ur (Rest House)	8	15
Baghdad—Hilla—Diwaniya—Semawa—Nasiriya—Basrah.	8	568
Baghdad—Mahmudiya—Babylon Junction	8	92
Babylon Junction—Babylon (Rest House)	—	1
Babylon Junction—Hilla	8	8
Hilla—Hindiya—Kerbala (Tourist Hotel)	—	42
Hilla—Hindiya Barrage (Rest House)	—	31
Hilla—Kufa—Najaf (Tourist Hotel)	—	61
Hilla—Hashimiya—Diwaniya (Tourist Hotel)	—	81
Diwaniya—Hamza—Semawa	8	89
Semawa—Warka (Uruk), unpaved.	8	65
Semawa—Khidhir	—	30
Khidhir—Warka (Uruk), unpaved.	8	24

Route		
Baghdad–Baquba–Derbendi Khan–Sulaimaniya.	4/5	333
Baghdad–Baquba–Saadiya	5	141
Saadiya–Jalawla	4	11
Jalawla–Derbendi Khan Dam Lake	4	117
Derbendi Khan–Arbat	4	43
Arbat–Sulaimaniya	4	21
Sulaimaniya–Sarchinar	–	5
Sulaimaniya–Dokan Junction–Kirkuk	4	110
Sulaimaniya–Dokan Junction (Tasluja).	4	20
Dokan Junction–Chamchamal	4	44
Chamchamal–Kirkuk	4	46
Baghdad–Ctesiphon (Al-Mada'in)	6	33
Baghdad–Kut–Amara–Basrah	6	549
Baghdad–Aziziya–Kut	6	170
Kut–Ali al-Gharbi (Restaurant)	6	94
Ali al-Gharbi–Amara (Rest House)	6	102
Amara–Qurna (Rest House)	6	108
Qurna–Basrah	6	74
Basrah–Abul Khasib (the old road)	–	2
Basrah–Abul Khasib (Restaurant & Rest House)		
Abul Khasib–Siba–Fao	6	26
Basrah (Margil)–Tannuma–Shlamcheh	6	80
Khidhir–Ur (Rest House), under construction.	8	60
Ur–Nasiriya (Rest House)	8	15
Nasiriya–Suq al-Shuyoukh	8	28
Suq al-Shuyoukh–Chebayish (the Marshes) (Tourist Cabins), unpaved	8	47
Nasiriya–Islah–Fuhoud (the Marshes), unpaved.	–	64
Fuhoud–Chebayish (the Marshes–Tourist Cabins), unpaved.	–	–
Chebayish–Madina–Qurna (Rest House)	8	44
Qurna–Basrah	6	74
Basrah–Zubair Junction–Safwan (on Kuwaiti border – Rest House).	8	50
Baghdad–Haswa–Musayib–Kerbala	8/9	103
Baghdad–Haswa	8	54
Haswa–Musayib	9	15
Musayib–Hindiya Barrage (Rest House).	–	9
Musayib–Kerbala (Tourist Hotel)	9	32
Kerbala–Razzazeh Lake	–	24
Razzazeh Lake–Shu'aib	–	26
Shu'aib–Ukhaidhir Castle (Rest House)	–	10
Shu'aib–Ain Tamr (Mineral water springs, Chalets, Restaurants).	–	25

AUTOMOBILE ROADS FOR TOURISTS

Name of Road	Road №	Distance in Kms.	Name of Road	Road №	Distance in Kms.
Kerbala—Najaf (Tourist Hotel)	9	78	(to Amman)	10	163
Najaf—Shamiya—Diwaniya (Tourist Hotel)	9	65	Rutba — H3 — Tunf (Syrian Border, thence to Damascus, Rest House)	10/11	170
Baghdad—Habbaniya—Rumadi—Rutba	10	410	Baghdad—Heet Junction—Qa'im—Syrian Border.	10/12	424
Baghdad—Falluja—Habbaniya	10	85			
Habbaniya Junction—Habbaniya Lake (Restaurant, Chalets, Tourist City)	—	5	Baghdad—Heet Junction	10	140
Habbaniya—Rumadi (Tourist Hotel)	10	25	Heet Junction—Heet	12	32
Rumadi—Heet Junction	10	30	Heet—Haditha (Rest House) — Ana — Qa'im (Rest House)	12	244
Heet Junction—Rutba (Tourist Hotel)	10	270	Qa'im—Syrian Border (thence to Aleppo)	12	8
Rutba — H3 — Jordanian Border					

DISTANCES TABLE BETWEEN THE GOVERNORATE CENTERS IN KILOMETERS

	DOHUK	MOSUL	ERBIL	SULAIMANIYA	TIKRIT	KIRKUK	BAQUBA	BAGHDAD	RAMADI	HILLA	KERBALA	KUT	NAJAF	NASIRIYA	AMARA	SAMAWA	DIWANIYA	BASRAH
DOHUK	—	69	153	355	290	248	531	465	575	565	583	637	626	840	831	735	646	1014
MOSUL	69	—	84	286	221	177	393	396	506	496	504	568	557	771	762	666	577	945
ERBIL	153	84	—	202	205	93	308	350	460	471	552	511	725	716	620	521		899
SULAIMANIYA	355	286	202	—	221	109	267	331	442	431	449	503	492	706	697	601	512	724
TIKRIT	290	221	205	221	—	112	241	175	285	275	293	347	336	550	541	445	467	804
KIRKUK	248	177	93	109	112	—	215	255	365	355	372	427	416	630	621	525	436	605
BAQUBA	531	393	308	267	241	215	—	66	176	166	184	238	227	441	432	336	247	605
BAGHDAD	465	396	350	331	175	255	66	—	110	100	108	172	161	375	366	271	181	549
RAMADI	575	506	460	442	285	365	176	110	—	210	218	292	271	485	476	380	291	659
HILLA	565	496	471	431	275	355	166	100	210	—	42	272	61	275	466	170	81	483
KERBALA	583	504	552	449	293	372	184	108	218	42	—	280	78	317	484	212	123	524
KUT	637	568	511	503	347	427	238	172	292	272	280	—	333	187	197	292	353	377
NAJAF	626	557	725	492	336	416	227	161	271	61	78	333	—	258	527	155	65	457
NASIRIYA	840	771	716	706	550	630	441	375	485	275	317	187	258	—	384	105	194	208
AMARA	831	762	620	697	541	621	432	366	476	466	484	197	527	384	—	489	546	182
SAMAWA	735	666	521	601	445	525	336	271	380	170	212	292	155	105	489	—	89	313
DIWANIYA	646	577		512	467	436	247	181	291	81	123	353	65	194	546	89	—	402
BASRAH	1014	945	899	724	804	605	605	549	659	483	524	377	457	208	182	313	402	—

215

TOURIST ESTABLISHMENTS OWNED BY THE SOCIALIST SECTOR

HOTELS:

Name	Class	Address	Telephone
Rashid	De luxe	Karkh, Baghdad.	
Palestine Meridien	De luxe	Sa'doun St., Baghdad.	
Ishtar Sheraton	De luxe	Baghdad.	
Babylon Obroi	De luxe	Jadiriya, Baghdad	
Mansour Melia	De luxe	Salhiya, Baghdad	30041 (10 lines)
Sadeer Novotel	De luxe	Andalusia Sq., Baghdad.	
Baghdad	Upper Super	Sa'doun St., Baghdad	8877041
Habbaniya Tourist Village (Hotel)	Lower Super	Anbar Governorate	8871984 771985 8871986 770050
Canal	Upper First	Canal St., Baghdad	
Kadhimiya	Lower First	Kadhimiya	4411427
Ibn Firnass	Lower First	International Airport Road.	551433 5520076
Arabian Gulf	Lower First	Basrah	212743

RESTAURANTS:

Name	Class	Address	Telephone
Asian	Lower Super	Hurriya Sq., Bagd.	7767467
Venice	Lower Super	Hurriya Sq., Bagd.	7767468
Shumoo'	Upper First	Sa'doun St., Bagd.	7767827
Khan Marjan	Upper First	Samawal St., Bagd.	8871444
Boats Wharf	Med. First	Abu Nuwas St., Bagd.	8882034
Sindbad Island	Lower First	Basrah	93708
Mada'in	Lower First	Ctesiphon	417109
Sarsang	Upper Second	Duhok Gov'te.	Ex. line 39
Inshki Cave	Upper Second	Inshki, Duhok Gov'te.	
Forests	Upper Second	Forests, Nineveh	818240
Salahuddin	Upper Second	Salahuddin, Arbil Governorate.	
Sara Rush	Upper Second	Salahuddin, Arbil Governorate.	Ex. line 86
Agargouf	Lower Second	Nr. Abu Ghraib, Bagd.	

TOURIST COMPLEXES:

Name	Class	Address	Telephone
Dokan	Lower Second	Sulaimaniya Gov'te.	44
Mada'in	Lower Second		

			2/055 21951/5
Sulaf	Lower First	Duhok Gov'te.	
Salam	Lower First	Najaf	331880
Howra	Lower First	Karbala	323262
Samarra	Lower First	Samarra	2837
Shaqlawa	Lower First	Shaqlawa	99022895
Mada'in Tourist Complex			
Najaf Tourist	Lower First	Ctesiphon	39
Rutba	Upper Second	Najaf	330358
	Upper Second	Rutba	Rutba Exchange 31279
Amara	Upper Second	Amara	
Kirkuk	Medium Second	Kirkuk	6614-6201
Gurna	Lower Second	Gurna, Basrah.	Ex. line 92
Safwan	Lower Second	Safwan, Basrah	Ex. line 10
Sarsang	Lower Second	Duhok Gov'te.	
Karbala Tourist	Lower Second	Karbala	321100
Agargouf	Lower Second	Nr. Abu Ghraib, Baghdad.	
Babylon	Lower Second	Babylon Site.	2200017
Old Sarsang	Med. Third	Duhok Gov'te.	
Nasiriya	Lower Third	Nasiriya	
Hatra	Lower Third	Hatra	
Diwaniya	Lower Third	Diwaniya	03662456
Ramadi	Lower Third	Ramadi	024422295
Um al-Qura	Special	Tikrit	021823091

TOURIST VILLAGES.

Swara Tuga		Duhok Gov'te	
Sarsang		Duhok Gov'te	
Salhuddin		Arbil Gov'te	
Sara Rush		Arbil Gov'te	
Shaqlawa		Arbil Gov'te	

TOURIST APARTMENTS:

Mada'in Super	Lower Super	Ctesiphon	Ex. line 39
Mada'in Medium	Lower Second	Karbala	28
Mada'in Small			
Sindbad Large	Lower First	Sindbad Island, Basrah.	417109
Sindbad Small	Upper Third	Ka-bala	28
Ain Tamr	Lower Second	Karbala	28
Inshki	Upper Third	Duhok Gov'te.	
Sulaf	Upper Third	Duhok Gov'te.	
Sara Rush	Medium Third	Arbil Gov'te.	

GAMES ROOMS:

Sara Rush	Third	Arbil Gov'te	261-250
Salahuddin	Lower Third	A-bil Gov'te	Ex. line 87
Sarsarg	Lower Third	Duhok Gove'te.	

217

TOURIST ESTABLISHMENTS OWNED BY THE SOCIALIST SECTOR

Name	Class	Address	Telephone		Name	Class	Address	Telephone
TOURIST CHALETS:					**CASINOS:**			
Nineveh Forest (large)	Upper Third	Nineveh	816500		Mada'in	Lower Second	Ctesiphon, Bagd.	Ex. line 39
Nineveh Forest (small)	Upper Fourth	Nineveh	811240		Ain Tamr	Med. Third	Karbala Gov'te.	
Waterfalls	Med. Fourth	Nineveh	811329		Abul Khasib	Lower Third	Basrah Gov'te.	
					Waterfalls	Lower Third	Nineveh	
					Lower Sulaf	Lower Third	Duhok Gov'te.	
SUPERMARKETS:					Tikrit		Salahuddin Gov'te.	021822005
Inshki		Duhok Gov'te.			Inshki Night Club	Upper Second	Duhok Gov'te.	

A SELECTED LIST OF HOTELS IN BAGHDAD

(Other than those listed under "Tourist Establishments owned by the Socialist Sector").

Name	Class	Address	Telephone		Name	Class	Address	Telephone
Shahin	Lower Super	Masbah			Orient Palace	Lower First	Masbah	96041
Petra	Upper First	Sa'doun St.	99035		Aswan	Lower First	Fateh Sq.	7761972
Diana	Upper First	Abu Nuwas St.	7762050		Abbasid Palace	Lower First	Sa'doun St.	7769910
Dar al-Salam	Upper First	Sa'doun St.	7766421		Saha	Lower First	Mansour	5513169
Baghdad Tower	Upper First	Masbah	96584		Sakhra (the Rock)	Lower First	Nidhal St.	7766381
Karma	Upper First	Jadiriya	7766926		Ramasese	Lower First	Battawivin	8882160

Name	Class	Address	Telephone
Oras	Medium First	Nidhal St.	
Casa Blanca	Medium First	Sa'doun St.	7766623
Agadir	Medium First	Sa'doun St.	93071
Andalusia Palace	Medium First	Sa'doun St.	7766428
Qadisiya	Medium First	Masbah	7761750
Muntazah	Lower First	Sa'doun St.	93080
Farabi	Lower First	Sa'doun St.	8872657
Khayam	Lower First	Sa'doun St.	7761971
Diwan	Lower First	Sa'doun St.	8889961
Abu Nuwas	Lower First	Abu Nuwas St.	99926
Adam	Lower First	Sa'doun St.	7766427
Ambassador	Lower First	Abu Nuwas St.	8874866
Local Tourist	Lower First	Harithiya	
Karawan	Upper Second	Nidhal St.	96091
Ara	Upper Second	Masbah	96421
Sahara	Upper Second	Andalusia Sq.	7764511
Nefertit	Upper Second	Masbah	96936
Babylon Palace	Upper Second	Nidhal St.	90091
Larsa	Upper Second	Sa'doun St.	91784
Muscat	Upper Second	Uqba bin Nafi Sq.	92313
Gilgamesh	Upper Second	Sa'doun St.	7764510
Zumurrud	Upper Second	Sa'doun St.	8870670
Qindeel	Upper Second	Nidhal St.	8873391/3
Binzert	Upper Second	Sa'doun St.	

CINEMAS IN BAGHDAD

Name	Address	Telephone
Babylon	Sa'doun St.	94473
Semiramis	Sa'doun St.	8883323 / 8887652
Nasr	Sa'doun St.	96562
Khayam	Khayam St.	8885909
Granada	Kifah St.	8882707

PUBLIC SWIMMING POOLS

Name / Address	Telephone
Adhamiya, Aouth Centre, Antar Sq.	26047
Kadhimiya, Zahra St.	21268
Amana Masbah	97082
Zawra Olympic, Zawra Park, 14th July St.	37278
People's International Stadium	7744194

A SHORT LIST OF SPORTS CLUBS IN BAGHDAD

	Telephone		Telephone
Iraqi Hunt Club, Mansour.	5513244	Karkh Sports Club, Mansour.	5511923
Iraqi Horsemanship Club,		Kadhimiya Sports Club, Industrial Area.	
The Office in Zawra Sports Club.	8884264	Sa'doun Sports Club, Nidhal St.	8880642
Zawra Sports Club,		Tammuz Sports Club, New Baghdad Road.	99252
Jaffa St., Karradat Mariam.	32268	Soli Chess Club, Yarmouk	5518064
Adhamiya Sports Club, Haibat Khatoun, Adhamiya	29219		

STADIUMS IN BAGHDAD

	Telephone		Telephone
People's International Stadium, Muthanna St.	7744194	Scouts Stadium, Al-Imam al-Adham St.	28403
		14th July Stadium, Mansour.	30478

NIGHT CLUBS IN BAGHDAD

	Telephone		Telephone
Lialina, Baghdad Hotel.	8877041	Local, Masbah.	92156
Moulin Rouge, Uqba bin Nafi Sq.	99848/90809	Al-Lie, Sa'doun St.	8873174
Thousand and One Nights, Sa'doun St.	91079	Nujoum, Sa'doun St.	8876411
The Ambassadors, Masbah.	92582	Hindiya, Masbah	

YOUTH HOSTELS IN IRAQ

Governorate	Address	Telephone	Governorate	Address	Telephone
Baghdad	Baghdad Youth Hostel, Sa'doun, Nidhal Quarter, 7/30/102.	97307	Diyala	Baquba, Local Administration. Stadium.	
Nineveh	Mosul, Rifat Haj Sirri St., Ghuzlani Quarter, 31/133/254.	5178	Missan	Amara. Qadiriya Quarter, Bustan Awasha.	
Ta'mim	Kirkuk, 23/112/Baghdad-Mansour Rd.	—	Najaf	Najaf, Sa'd Quarter, 3188/293.	
Babylon	Hilla, Babylon Quarier, 215/12	220905	Karbala	Karbala, Baghdad Gate.	20177
Wasit	Kut, 30th July Quarter, 28/154/42/14.				

MUSEUMS IN IRAQ

Museum	Telephone
Iraq Museum, Museum Sq., Karkh, Baghdad.	
Museum of Iraqi Art Pioneers, Rashid Street, Baghdad.	8872800
Popular Costume and Folklore Museum, Sinak, Rashid St. Baghdad.	3886876
Museum of National History, North Gate, Baghdad.	65790
Arab Ba'th Socialist Party Museum, Ali Saleh, 14th July St., Baghdad.	4411911
College of Arts Museum, College of Arts, Waziriya, Baghdad.	68151
Baghdadi Museum, Mamoun St., near Shuhada Bridge, Baghdad.	8885317
Wastani (Dhafariya) Gate Museum, Sheikh Omar St., Baghdad.	62636
War Museum, Kasrah, Adhamiya Park, Baghdad.	28641
Agargouf Museum, On the site, Baghdad.	
National Museum of Modern Art, Kifah Street, Tayaran Sq., Baghdad.	8874221

MUSEUMS IN IRAQ

	Telephone
Mustansiriya School Museum, Mustansiriya, Rusafa, Baghdad.	8885765
Abbasid Palace Museum, Abbasid Palace, Rusafa, Baghdad.	8884950
Mosul Museum, near Hurriya Bridge.	2420
Nirgal Gate Museum, Mosul, Nineveh Remains.	
Natural History Museum, University of Mosul, near Shuhada Park.	
Mosul University Folklore Museum, Old Museum, Mosul.	
The Mosul House, Sarikhana, near Na'maniya Mosque, Mosul.	

	Telephone
Basrah Museum, Basrah.	318498
Museum of the 1920 Revolution, Hai Quarter, Najaf.	31604
Nasiriya Museum, Nasriya.	
Babylon Museum, On the site.	223080
Anbar Museum, Ramadi.	
Samarra Museum, Samarra.	
Ta'mim Museum, Kirkuk.	212102
Sulaimaniya Museum, Sulaimaniya.	20609
Arbil Museum, Arbil.	21745

SOME TAXI CAB OFFICES IN BAGHDAD

Name of Office	Address	Telephone	Name of Office	Address	Telephone
Saad	$\frac{6}{2}$/82/609 Wihda Quarter.	90982	Sumer	2/1/164 Alwiya Quarter.	92143
Baghdad Car	$\frac{42}{2}$/2/929 Babylon Quarter.	97721	Zuhair	$\frac{22}{6}$/5/929 Babylon Quarter.	97985
Tourist	1/1/903 Karrada Quarter.	95662	Babylon	$\frac{27}{3}$/77/903 Karrada Quarter.	99194
Sindbad	$\frac{119}{1}$/38/903 Karrada Quarter.	92964	Ghazi	66/906 Wihda Quarter.	93554
Rafidain	20/1 Walid St., Wihda Quarter.	92854	Nineveh	Sa'doun St. (Opp. Agadir Hotel).	
Diana Car	53/9/929, Wihda Quarter.	98433			

AIRLINES OPERATING IN IRAQ

Note: All the following airlines have their main offices in Sa'doun St., Baghdad.

	Telephone		Telephone
Iraqi Airways, Sa'doun St.	887005	Swiss Airlines.	88873261, 91937
Iraqi Airways, Rashid St.	8883416	Soviet Airlines. (Aeroflot).	8881250
Iraqi Airways, Adhamiya.	22621	Finnish Airlines.	8874516, 8875880
Iraqi Airways, Mansour.	5521668	Air France.	8876624, 8872751
Pakistani Airways.	8887181	Kuwaiti Airlines.	8886337, 8888018
British Airways.	8886446, 8883534	Middle East Airlines.	8873271, 8871724
Bulgarian Airways.	8888978	Hungarian Airlines.	8889233
Belgian Airways.	8882276, 96631	Air India.	8880641
Polish Airways.	8881314	Dutch Airlines.	8871956
Turkish Airways.	8884755	Japanese Airlines.	8875181, 8875047
Czechoslovak Airways.	8871662, 8871972	Alitalia.	8887095, 8889741
Gulf Air.	8877566, 8881146	Yugoslav Airlines.	886168
Jordanian Airways (Alia).	8885358, 8884299	Lufthansa.	8885457, 8889771
Saudi Airways.	8881269, 8883554	Interflug (German Democratic Airlires).	888978, 8889780
Scandinavian Airlines.	8888238		

* * *

With Compliments of
The State Organization For Tourism

BAGHDAD—IRAQ

Compiled, photographed and issued by
The Promotion Section in the General
Establishment for Travel and Tourism Services
BAGHDAD — IRAQ
Telex — 2781 GETTS IK
Phone: 7760026
P.O.Box 10028 KARRADH

Layout: YUGOSLAVIAPUBLIC, Beograd, Knez-Mihailova 10
Telex 11125 and 11431 YU YUPUB ● Phone: 633-266

Printed in Yugoslavia: YUGOSLAVIAPUBLIC, Beograd —
Mladinska knjiga, Ljubljana